DAVID G. GALLAUGHER

ANY OLD TIME BOOK 5

Paul Borthwick

VICTOR BOOKS
A DIVISION OF SCRIPTURE PRESS PUBLICATIONS INC.
USA CANADA ENGLAND

Scripture taken from the *Holy Bible, New International Version,* © 1973, 1978, 1984, International Bible Society. Used by permission of Zondervan Bible Publishers. Other Scripture quotations are from *New American Standard Bible* (NASB), © the Lockman Foundation 1960, 1962, 1963, 1968, 1971, 1972, 1973, 1975, 1977.

3 4 5 6 7 8 9 10 Printing/Year 94 93 92 91 90

Library of Congress Catalog Card Number: 84-50233
ISBN: 0-89693-187-0
© 1986 by SP Publications, Inc. All rights reserved
Printed in the United States of America

CONTENTS

Page

SECTION 1 STRATEGY FOR OUTREACH

7	Session 1	SEEING PEOPLE FROM GOD'S PERSPECTIVE (Vision) Who does God think *you* are?	John 4:1-26
11	Session 2	REACHING THE PEOPLE YOU KNOW (Friendship evangelism) How can I touch my friends?	Selected passages
15	Session 3	REJECTED—BUT NOT BY ME! (Caring for outcasts) How can I care for people that no one likes?	Selected passages
19	Session 4	GET TO THE POINT! (Personal evangelism) How can I bring conversations around to Christ?	John 3

SECTION 2 INTO THE NEIGHBORHOOD

25	Session 5	SHARING MY LOCKER WITH JESUS (Outreach at school) Can Jesus go to school with me?	Hebrews 13:5
29	Session 6	I'LL GO ANYWHERE—BUT NEXT DOOR (Outreach in the neighborhood) How can I witness to my neighbor?	Selected passages
33	Session 7	TAKING GOLD TO THE GOLDEN-AGERS (Outreach to the elderly) Do old people really need me?	Selected passages
37	Session 8	GOING TO TOWN WITH JESUS (Outreach in the community) How can I affect my town for Christ?	Selected passages

SECTION 3 BEHIND THE BARRIERS

43	Session 9	I'M OK, BUT WHAT ABOUT YOU? (Across ethnic barriers) How can I reach out to people who are different than I?	Selected passages
48	Session 10	BUT WE'VE ALWAYS DONE IT THIS WAY! (Across cultural barriers) How come people are so different?	Acts 10:9-48
52	Session 11	AND YOU VISITED ME! (Serving the poor) Can I really serve Jesus in person?	Matthew 25:31-46
56	Session 12	LEPERS—IN MY WORLD? (Across social barriers) How can I help the really hurting person?	Selected passages

SECTION 4 TO THE ENDS OF THE EARTH

63	Session 13	EXPAND YOUR HORIZONS (Building a worldview) What do I have to do with the big world?	Selected passages
68	Session 14	MISSIONS—A DAILY AFFAIR (Personalizing missions) How does world missions apply to my life?	Selected passages
72	Session 15	BUT I DON'T CARE WHERE BURKINA FASO IS (Building compassion) Missions is so vast—how can I care about it all?	Selected passages
77	Session 16	MY ROLE IN THE WORLD (Personal response) Where does God want me to go?	Jonah

HOW TO USE AN *ANY OLD TIME*

SonPower *Any Old Times* (AOTs) are designed to meet a need expressed by many youth leaders—to have a series of topical, self-contained meeting ideas in a format that will "plug in" to their existing programs. Each AOT session is biblical, easy to use, and requires minimal preparation. This book of *Any Old Times* is geared to high school teens, but every session has suggestions for adapting the material to a junior high level.

Each basic session is compact (about 45 minutes) so it can be used "any old time"—after a hayride, on a retreat, during your regular youth group meeting, or just about anywhere. But all sessions can be expanded by using the optional activities included—games, suggestions for further study, additional resources, and so forth. (Optional activities are shaded throughout this book.)

Every AOT session contains three sections: an exercise or activity to arouse the teens' interest in the topic *(Warm-up)*, a biblical examination of the subject with discussion questions and/or other activities *(Workout)*, and a time for student response *(Wrap-up)*. The first page of each session highlights the session goal and provides other necessary information you will need to get started.

SPECIAL FEATURES

Summary page
The first page of each session will show you at a glance the key concept of the session, the goal, a short overview, the estimated time required, any materials or preparation needed, and tips for adapting the session to a junior high age-group.

Topical format
If you want to highlight a particular topic of study, AOTS provide a variety of creative, ready-to-use ideas.

Tips for leaders
The outside columns of the AOT sessions contain helpful hints as you lead the session. You should also find enough room for notes of your own.

Boldface type
The material printed in boldface can be read aloud. Of course, you don't need to read word for word. You should adapt these sections to fit your own unique style of teaching. But the bold type will help guide you through the sections where you will be speaking.

Shaded activities
Any parts of a session that are shaded are optional. These sections can be integrated into the session or skipped, depending on the amount of time you have. You know your specific group better than anyone else, so use your own discretion in using these optional activities.

Adaptability
This is probably the biggest benefit of *Any Old Times*. Each session can be easily adapted to fit your specific time frame, age-group, and meeting format. AOTS can be as flexible as you want them to be.

SECTION 1

STRATEGY FOR OUTREACH

One of the greatest errors that often accompanies a thrust toward world mission is the tendency to overlook the needs and opportunities that are right in front of us. Many people fall prey to what author Eugene Peterson calls "Afghanistanitus," the belief that all of the real needs are beyond our reach.

This section is designed to get students thinking about the people right around them. It builds on the foundation of seeing people from God's perspective and guides young people to start reaching out to friends, as well as to the unpopular kids at school. The concluding session covers what needs to be said when the Gospel is presented.

To teach these four sessions as a unit, you might begin by asking some basic questions of your students:
- Why do you think that many Christians never witness?
- Who do you think might be the most needy students at your school in need of God's love?
- What makes it tough to talk to your friends about Jesus?

Answers to these questions usually reveal that youth group members agree that Christians should be reaching out to others, but they feel nervous or unwilling to do it for themselves. With this realization in mind, you are ready to start the sessions on "Strategy for Outreach."

STRATEGY FOR OUTREACH

VISION   JOHN 4:1-26

SESSION 1

SEEING PEOPLE FROM GOD'S PERSPECTIVE

WHO DOES GOD THINK *YOU* ARE?

KEY CONCEPT — Outreach depends on our seeing other people the way that God sees them.

GOAL — This session will help students realize that every person is loved by and precious to God.

OVERVIEW — We all tend to ignore or even criticize people who are not part of our peer group, but such alienation is especially true among teenagers. While belonging is vitally important to each of them, they are still very slow to reach out to new people. This session will show that such hesitancy is normal but must be overcome by seeing people the way that God sees them.

TIME REQUIRED — 45-55 minutes

MATERIALS CHECKLIST —
Materials needed for basic session:
___ Bibles
___ Pens and paper *(Wrap-up)*
___ Handout *(Identification Game)*

Materials needed for optional openers:
___ Chalkboard and chalk or newsprint and pens *(Graffiti Board)*

JUNIOR HIGH ADAPTATION — Most of this session is immediately transferable for use with junior highers, though you should preview the session to modify some vocabulary that they may not know. Also, the extra study of Psalm 139 *(Options for Further Study)* is more important for junior highers who are often entering into a deep struggle regarding self-worth and self-acceptance.

TIPS FOR LEADERS

Try to use current examples, such as a television commercial in which one product is claimed to be superior to another.

As an opener, you may want to use the "Prui" game first because it is the most active.

SESSION OUTLINE

WARM-UP

Optional Openers (choose one)

Graffiti Board (10 minutes)

Using a chalkboard or a long piece of paper taped to the wall, get students to respond to this question: "What current examples can you cite of people feeling good about themselves by defeating someone else?" You may want to prime the pump with examples of politics, sports, or advertising. You may want to refer back to this later in the meeting, so leave up the recorded answers.

Prui (10-15 minutes)

This game illustrates the infectious magnetism of reaching out, but you should not cite this point until after the game is played. The Prui (pronounced PROO-ee) is a gentle, friendly creature that grows. If you want to get people in touch (literally) and feeling comfortable with each other, introduce them to the Prui.

Unlike the Blob, which everyone avoids, everybody wants to find and become part of the Prui. To do this, everyone stands in a group, closes their eyes, and starts milling about. When you bump into someone, shake his hand and ask, "Prui?" If the other person asks "Prui?" back, then you have *not* found the Prui. Keeping your eyes closed, find another person to ask.

When everybody is bumping about, shaking hands, with strains of "Prui? Prui? Prui?" floating around the crowd, the referee whispers to one of the players that she is the Prui. Since the Prui can see, she opens her eyes. It seems that the Prui is also a smiling mute, for when someone bumps into her, shakes her hand, and asks that gentle question, she doesn't respond. Ask again, just to make sure: "Prui?" No response. Eureka, you've found the Prui at last!

Now you can open your eyes—you're part of the Prui too. Keep holding the Prui's hand, and when someone bumps into you, shake with your free hand and don't respond when he asks. That's how the Prui grows.

You can only shake the Prui's hand at either end, so if you bump into two clasped hands, you know you've got the Prui somewhere in the middle. Feel your way to the end and join it.

Soon enough, everybody's happily holding hands except one or two lost souls groping their way along the line of bodies. When the last stray joins up and opens his eyes, the smiling Prui usually breaks the silence by letting out a spontaneous cheer.

("Prui" from *The New Games Book* by Andrew Fluegelman. Copyright © 1976 by Headlands Press, Inc. Reprinted by permission of Doubleday & Company, Inc.)

Identification Game (5-10 minutes)

Start by saying: **In our culture, we often discover that we do not feel so good about ourselves (the way we look, our performance, etc.). To overcompensate for our low feelings, we put other people down by criticizing or making fun of them. Sociologists call this action by technical names ending in "ism" that refer to the people or group being downgraded. Can you figure out these technical names?**

Discriminating against a young or old person (ageism).
Putting people down because of their ethnic background ("ethnism").

SESSION OUTLINE | TIPS FOR LEADERS

Thinking or acting unkindly toward the other gender (sexism).
Defaming people because of their economic status (classism).
Ridiculing or hurting people because of their race (racism).

After sharing the answers, discuss recent examples your students have seen (or done themselves!) that are manifestations of these "isms." At this point, just listen to examples without passing judgment. Let the Bible study do the judging.

WORKOUT

Read and Respond (20 minutes)

Say: **Jesus confronted all of these types of judgmental attitudes when He walked the earth. One of the most prominent examples occurs in John 4.** Read these passages one at a time and ask the following questions:

1. John 4:1-4
Jesus had to pass through Samaria. Does anyone know what would be difficult about Jesus, a Jew, going through the region of Samaria? (Samaritans were half Jew and half Gentile, and the Jews hated them.)

2. John 4:5-9
Why is it unusual that Jesus spoke to the Samaritan woman? (First, she was a Samaritan, and Jews and Samaritans did not talk. Second, she was a woman, and men and women of that time did not just "strike up conversations.")

What is unusual about the time of day for the woman to be drawing water at a well? (It was a desert-like area, and to be coming to a well at noon was most unusual. Most people would come to a well to draw water early in the day before it was hot. The woman here obviously was coming at an unusual time to avoid seeing other people, especially since the regular time for going to the well was also a social time for the village women.)

3. John 4:10-15
Jesus talked about living water and the woman talked about regular water. Why do you think that the woman didn't seem to get the message? (Jesus seemed to talk in codes that she didn't understand.)

4. John 4:16-19
To continue to explain things to this woman, Jesus changed the subject to her marital status. Why do you think Jesus did this? (He wanted her to confront her sin, and He wanted to let her know that He knew why she was coming to the well at an odd hour—because her marriage record and her current live-in lover would have made her the subject of others' gossip.)

5. John 4:20-26
Why do you think the woman started to change the subject? (She probably felt that Jesus was getting too personal with His questions about her husbands.)

Jesus told the woman about worship being related to the worshiper rather than the place. How might this apply to us? (It reminds us that worship is not restricted to church services or buildings.)

The woman stated her understanding of a coming Messiah. Jesus revealed Himself as that Messiah. What does it say about Jesus that He would present Himself as the Messiah to this woman? (It shows that He is the Saviour [Messiah] of all people, and He looks at people based on their need for "living water" [eternal life] rather than on their gender, racial or ethnic backgrounds, or even their sinful pasts.)

Tips sidebar:

You can add to this game by having students make up their own "isms" like "nerd-ism" or "grades-ism."

You might also point out here that Jesus' trip through Samaria was unusual. Most Jews would have taken an extra two-day trip out of their way to the east to avoid Samaria and the Samaritan people.

TIPS FOR LEADERS | SESSION OUTLINE

WRAP-UP

Summary (10 minutes)

Say: **As we watch Jesus relate to the Samaritan woman at the well, we learn several things about the way that God relates to and sees us.**

Using a personal testimony might be effective at this point.

Lesson 1: **God sees us as valuable and in need of His love despite our past. Jesus identified the sin of the woman (her adulterous lifestyle), but He never rejected her based on her past sins. He presented Himself as the Saviour/Messiah, regardless of her past.** One effective exercise at this point helps students realize that God will forgive their sins. Pass out pens and paper and have group members write down (privately) what they think is their worst sin or sins. Then tell them that if Jesus is their Saviour, God sees Jesus—not their sins. Have them write the name "Jesus" over their sin list. Because of Jesus, they can crumple the paper up and throw it away!

Try to add illustrations (getting cut from a sports team, failing a class, etc.) that your students can identify with.

Lesson 2: **God does not love us based on the standards of a sinful society. We might feel like losers (like the woman, who came to the well alone because she had no friends), or we might feel judged because of something like our race or gender or ethnic background. God sees us as we are and loves us without respect to our backgrounds.**

Lesson 3: **When we realize that God's love for us is not based on our backgrounds and that He forgives our sins, we can start to see ourselves and other people from God's perspective. He sees us all as in need of the Saviour Jesus, and He sees us all as precious and valuable.** Have students think of or list a "Samaritan woman-type" person in their lives whom they need to start reaching out to. Instruct them to think about a person they have not regarded as valuable, and challenge them to start seeing that person as God does.

Closing with a time of conversational prayer is helpful, especially if students are willing to confess before God that they have not been seeing themselves as He sees them. Thanking God for sending Jesus for us—in spite of ourselves—and asking God for power to reach out to people we have not been loving reminds students that outreach is based on seeing ourselves and others from God's perspective.

Options for Further Study

Option 1—It might be useful to supplement this session with a study of Psalm 139 to give your students a better perspective on their special place in God's eyes.

Option 2—Follow up next week by asking students how they did on their outreach efforts with the person they listed or thought of under Lesson 3 of *Wrap-up*.

Additional Resources

Fearfully and Wonderfully Made (Philip Yancey and Paul Brand, Zondervan)
Reinforces the specialness of each individual before God.

The Majesty of Man (Ronald Allen, Multnomah)
Addresses the issue of our special privilege of being the highest of God's creation.

Why Am I Afraid to Love? (John Powell, Argus)
Builds on the teaching that we must understand God's love for us *before* we love others.

STRATEGY FOR OUTREACH

FRIENDSHIP EVANGELISM   SELECTED PASSAGES

SESSION 2

REACHING THE PEOPLE YOU KNOW

HOW CAN I TOUCH MY FRIENDS?

KEY CONCEPT | Outreach should start right where we live.

GOAL | This session challenges young people to start reaching out to their closest peers.

OVERVIEW | It is all too easy to define outreach in terms of activities "over there" like missions. To understand outreach properly, however, students must see that reaching the people they already know—friends, neighbors, locker-mates, etc.—is their first responsibility before God.

TIME REQUIRED | 50-65 minutes

MATERIALS CHECKLIST | Materials needed for basic session:
____ Handout (*Friendship Evangelism Questionnaire*)
____ Pens
____ Bibles
____ Handout (*Friendship Evangelism Action Response*)

Materials needed for optional activities:
____ Chalkboard and chalk

JUNIOR HIGH ADAPTATION | Though "friendship evangelism" may sound pretty intimidating to junior highers, they can still learn from this session to start caring about nonbelievers right around them by praying for them. The *Friendship Evangelism Action Response* may need to be revised, and the second optional warm-up (*Discussion Starter*) is probably best left out.

TIPS FOR LEADERS | SESSION OUTLINE

WARM-UP

Optional Openers (choose one)

Debates (10 minutes)

Tip: You could use the Keith Green tract "Why You Should Go to the Mission Field" as part of your debate start-up.

Using an agree/disagree format, ask students to respond to this statement: "In light of the fact that God wants to reach the whole world with the love of Christ, and in light of the fact that most of the people who have *never* heard of Jesus are in India, China, and Muslim countries, every American Christian should plan to be a missionary."

After students decide whether they agree or disagree, get them into two groups to debate with each other in an effort to win people to their side. If one position is not taken, then you take it. Groups can use statistics, the Bible, and opinions in an effort to defend their views.

Discussion Starter (5-10 minutes)

Tip: Add here an example or two of people you know who love "the world" but hate their neighbors.

Say: **In John Updike's novel *The Coup*, an embassy official dies after trying to deliver food to a starving nation in Africa. His wife remembers him as "always helping people, although he only liked to help people he didn't know."** Using a chalkboard on which to record their responses, ask students: **Why do you think it is easier to help and care for people we don't know than it is to reach out to and care for those right near us?**

Friendship Evangelism Questionnaire (10-15 minutes)

Pass out this survey to your students and ask them to complete it and tally their scores.

Friendship Evangelism Questionnaire

1. List three people you consider your closest friends (outside of your youth group or your family):
   1. _____
   2. _____
   3. _____

   Score 10 points per friend   a. _____

2. Of these three, how many . . .
   know that you are a Christian? _____
   have you ever invited to church? _____
   know that you read the Bible? _____
   have you invited to youth group? _____
   have you directly witnessed to? _____

   Total _____ x 10 points each   b. _____

3. Of these friends, how many are already Christians? _____
   Deduct 20 points per Christian friend   c. _____

   Your Friendship Evangelism Quotient (a + b − c)   _____

Tip: Have a coleader collect these so that you are not distracted from moving on to the Workout.

You may or may not want to collect these. The feedback from the group should tell you who—if any—in your youth group has nonbelieving friends that they are trying to witness to. Close this opener by discussing for two to three minutes: **What do you think it says about us if all of our closest friends are already Christians? How can we start making friends with non-Christians?**

SESSION OUTLINE | TIPS FOR LEADERS

WORKOUT

Twentieth-Century Update (15-20 minutes)

Have your youth group break into small groups, and then assign them the task of reading and "updating" the following passages:

- Group 1—Mark 5:1-20
  Compose a skit in which a professional actor's agent discusses the story with the healed demoniac. The agent should reiterate what happened, and suggest speaking, writing, acting, and other options that are now open to the man. The skit should close with the healed demoniac making a decision based on verse 19.

- Group 2—Matthew 9:9-13
  Write an article about Jesus and Matthew for the *National Inquirer*. Include the response of Jesus and the author's opinions of why Jesus did what He did.

- Group 3—Matthew 4:18-20
  Bring this up to date with a skit that shows some modern equivalents of what it means to be "fishers of men." Remember to find contemporary jobs for the ones who are called and show what happens when they leave their jobs "immediately."

- Group 4—John 1:35-42
  Conduct a "man-on-the-street" interview with Andrew. Ask him questions about Jesus, the words of John, and why he went first after his brother, Simon Peter.

One adult leader per group is recommended, if possible.

Talk-to (5 minutes)

Say: **We sometimes think that the task of reaching out belongs to the missionary or the pastor. We can even find ourselves being more concerned about the world's starving people than we are about the people we call our best friends. Like the man we talked about earlier** *(Discussion Starter),* **we can find ourselves caring only about people we don't know.**

The example of Jesus and the people who followed Him was that they went first to the people right around them:
1. **The healed demoniac was told to go to his own people and tell them what the Lord did.**
2. **Andrew went immediately to his brother, Simon Peter.**
3. **Jesus encouraged Matthew to bring his friends together so He could be with them, even though they were despised in society.**
4. **Peter and Andrew and James and John were called by Jesus to be "fishers of men," to extend their "nets" to the people around them and bring them in to Jesus.**

We too must start where we are—reaching out to the people around us.

WRAP-UP (15 minutes)

Say: **Now that we have looked at Jesus and the others who started reaching out by going first to the people they knew, we need to think about ourselves.**

Added illustrations out of your own life greatly enhance the points you have just made and prepare students to apply the truths themselves.

Friendship Evangelism Action Response

Have students fill out once again a Friendship Evangelism Questionnaire, only this time it should be called the Friendship Evangelism Action Response (below). After these responses are completed you could close in prayer or you could—before you pray—have someone (whom you asked before the meeting) give a testimony of how God has used him or her in a friendship evangelism role.

Friendship Evangelism Action Response

List three people you are friendly with who are—to the best of your knowledge—not Christians:

1. _____
2. _____
3. _____

Your Action Response is threefold:
PRAY: Will you commit yourself to pray every day for the next week (month, or some time you determine) for these three friends? _____
PREPARE: To get ready to share Christ with your friends, will you do any of the following?
_____ Read about evangelism
_____ Learn how to use an evangelistic booklet
_____ Join an evangelism training class
PURSUE: To go after your friends, what action will you take to start reaching out to them?
_____ Invite them to youth group
_____ Invite them to a church service
_____ Pay a special visit to them
_____ Invite them to your home—just to build your friendship

Option for Further Study

This session can be used to prepare for what is called an "Andrew Dinner." Using the example of Andrew in John 1, you can encourage students to start praying about and pursuing a "Simon" that they can invite to a dinner sponsored by the youth group. Like Andrew, your students' role will be to bring people to a place where they can be introduced to Jesus (through the program and speaker surrounding the dinner).

Additional Resources

Ordinary Guy (Day Star Productions)
A good film introducing the fact that God uses ordinary people to do His work.

Friendship Evangelism (Arthur McPhee, Zondervan)
Discusses the best approaches for winning friends to Christ.

Four Spiritual Laws (Campus Crusade for Christ) and other booklets like it can be introduced in this session as well as in session 4 to give students a practical tool to help them share with their friends.

Dare to Be Different (Fred Hartley, Revell)
Written for young people on the challenge of overcoming peer pressure.

Real Friends (Barbara Varenhorst, Harper and Row)
Helps students build deeper relationships based on caring which can provide excellent opportunities for witness.

STRATEGY FOR OUTREACH

CARING FOR OUTCASTS   SELECTED PASSAGES

SESSION 3

REJECTED—BUT NOT BY ME!

HOW CAN I CARE FOR PEOPLE THAT NO ONE LIKES?

KEY CONCEPT | We must overcome the labels that keep us from caring for certain people.

GOAL | The challenge of this session is for group members to break down stereotypes and reach out to those labeled "outcasts."

OVERVIEW | For any number of reasons, students label others as rejects, "nerds," or outcasts. Whether because of personality, physical size, looks, or even handicaps, there are always those that are left out of the "in" group. This session challenges such unfair stereotyping and criticism and opens the door for effective outreach into the lives of your group's or community's most hurting young people.

TIME REQUIRED | 55-70 minutes

MATERIALS CHECKLIST | Materials needed for basic session:
___ Bibles
___ Pens and paper
___ A sample repentance response written out

Materials needed for optional activities:
___ Prize (*"Moo" Game*)

JUNIOR HIGH ADAPTATION | This session is very significant for junior highers who are often ruthless in criticizing and rejecting their peers. It is probably best to eliminate *Loser Line-up* and *The "Moo" Game* altogether because these can easily get out of hand and give way to cutting remarks about others. The Abe Lincoln story is effective, however, and the Bible study is transferable. In the repentance exercise, make sure to assist students with some practical and tangible ways that they can begin loving people they do not like. You may even want to start with negative applications like, "I will stop laughing at . . ." because this is the level at which most of them really live.

| TIPS FOR LEADERS | SESSION OUTLINE |

WARM-UP

Optional Openers

Loser Line-up (10 minutes)

Though we do not like to admit it (and we certainly do not want to reinforce it), all of our students hold certain stereotypes about what makes a fellow student a loser. Get into small groups in which one or two members have to be part of the loser line-up. Participants in the line-up must speak of or act out some behavior or external characteristic that leads to someone's being called a loser or reject at school. (You may generate ideas by suggesting things like carrying a briefcase or wearing out-of-date clothes, but caution students against using any one individual as the target of their humor. Remind them that we want to laugh at funny behaviors, not specific people.)

The "Moo" Game (10 minutes)

Choose one of your stronger students to be the one laughed at in this game.

This is a good game for helping students know what it's like to be an outcast. One student is selected as the judge, and he leaves the room. Outside the room the instructions are given; his job is to pick out the one student who "moos" the loudest on cue. He is told that all students will be mooing but only one will be extra loud. At the same time as these instructions are being given, one other student is taken out into another room and told that he will be the one "mooing" the loudest and that he must "moo" at the top of his lungs because the others will be "mooing" too. Simultaneous with these two sets of instructions, the rest of the students are instructed that on the signal to "moo," they are to remain silent.

Both students are ushered back in, and the leader reiterates the rules about "mooing" so as to cover the one "mooing" the loudest. On the signal, the loud "moo-er" will let out an enormous bellow—all alone, to the mocking glee of the rest of the group.

Rewarding this student with a prize for being a good sport can help offset any ill effects of this game.

After the embarrassment, ask the student who made a fool of himself what it felt like to be all alone, thinking that everyone was laughing at him.

Discussion Starter (10 minutes)

Read the following story about the events in the life of Abraham Lincoln. Before you tell students who the person described is, ask them how they would have responded to this man. Try to help them see that all of us make judgments based on external failures which make us treat people unfairly.

Say: **How would you predict the future of a man who:**
- **grew up on an isolated farm?**
- **had only one year of formal education?**
- **read fewer than 10 books in his youth?**
- **lost his job?**
- **was defeated for political offices (both local and federal) a total of seven times?**
- **failed in business?**
- **suffered the loss of his sweetheart?**
- **experienced a nervous breakdown?**
- **was rejected for a federal job?**

Would you call such a man a loser? Most of us would. Yet to write people off as losers or failures is not God's way at all, for in 1860 this "failure" was elected President of the United States. Abraham Lincoln went on to be one of the godliest and greatest Presidents our country has ever known.

SESSION OUTLINE | TIPS FOR LEADERS

After discussing our tendency to stereotype people as failures or losers, read the following quotation. (Taken from *The Pursuit of Excellence*. Copyright © 1982 by The Zondervan Corporation. Used by permission.)

Think, for example, of Abraham Lincoln, who was elected president of the United States in 1860. He grew up on an isolated farm and had only one year of formal education. In those early years, he was exposed to barely half a dozen books. In 1832 he lost his job and was defeated in the race for the Illinois legislature. In 1833 he failed in business. In 1834 he was elected to the state legislature, but in 1835 his sweetheart died, and in 1836 he had a nervous breakdown. In 1838 he was defeated for Speaker of the House, and in 1843 he was defeated for nomination for Congress. In 1846 he was elected to Congress but in 1848 lost the renomination. In 1849 he was rejected for a federal land officer appointment, and in 1854 he was defeated for the Senate. In 1856 he was defeated for the nomination of vice president, and in 1858 he was again defeated for the Senate.

Many people, both at home and abroad, consider Lincoln to be the greatest president of all time. Yet it should be remembered how many failures and defeats marked his life and how humble and unpromising his early beginnings were.

WORKOUT

Discussion Groups (10-15 minutes)

One adult leader per discussion group is ideal.

The Bible is full of examples of God's concern for the person that no one likes. Divide into three groups to examine different Scriptures related to God's love of the rejected person. After discussion, have a representative from each group give a summary report. Suggestions for discussion are in parentheses.
• *Group 1*—Leviticus 19:13-18, 33-34 (The basic Old Testament laws addressed the ways that God wanted His people to relate both to each other and to outsiders. The foundational command is to "love your neighbor as yourself" (v. 18), and this has practical outworkings in kind treatment to the handicapped, hospitality to strangers, and fairness and honesty with neighbors.)
• *Group 2*—1 Corinthians 13:1-13 (Note that the description of love is action-oriented and not based on feelings. The love that we are to show to others requires us to demonstrate kindness, patience, and other qualities, regardless of the beauty, popularity, or likeability of the person being loved. A good cross-reference is Romans 5:8; God did not *like* us because we were sinners, but He still demonstrated *love* to us.)
• *Group 3*—Isaiah 61:1-3 [Luke 4:18-19 refers to this passage.] (Here the description of the Messiah's activities are directed toward those who might be outcasts or rejects by society's standards—the afflicted and the brokenhearted, the prisoners, and the captives. The Messiah's special concern would be for those who were the "down-and-out" of society.)

Your illustrations of action love versus popular love can help students distinguish godly love from their emotional, feeling-oriented love.

Talk-to (5 minutes)

Say: **We all have the tendency to ignore the person that no one likes. We may simply stay away from people like this, or we may even join right in with others in ridiculing or teasing such people. As Christians, we must recognize first and foremost that this rejection of others is sinful and that it discredits us as witnesses of the love of Christ. Second, we must realize that God's love toward us is not based on the fact that He likes us, but on the fact that He chose to act in love toward us.**

This is a very tough statement, especially to teenagers whose identities are linked to their cliques and to the people they reject. It might bear repeating.

One of the greatest challenges facing a teenager in high school is to be a Christian—in word and deed—toward the rejected, unpopular student.

TIPS FOR LEADERS | SESSION OUTLINE

We do not have to wait until we feel love or until we start liking the person. Actually, our feelings have very little to do with it. Instead, we must start showing our love toward others by demonstrations of kindness and actions of love.

If we are to be effective as disciples of Christ, we must repent of our bad attitudes and start loving even the unpopular students around us.

WRAP-UP

Repentance (10 minutes)

Say: **Repentance literally means a turn-about-face, a 180-degree change of direction. When we repent, we say in effect, "God, the direction I have been headed is the wrong way, and I am willing to turn around and head in the other direction."**

Have a sample repentance sheet prepared to show students, or put a sample on the chalkboard or on an overhead transparency.

Then have students (individually) write on a piece of paper names of two students they really don't like. Have them draw an arrow representing themselves going away from these students' names (representing themselves and their rejecting attitudes). Tell them then to stop the arrow and reverse the direction (now going back toward the two students' names). Have them mark the turn in the arrow "repentance." Below the arrow (now directed toward the students' names), have your group members write two or three actions that they will take *this week* to demonstrate God's love to these two students.

Testimony (5 minutes)

The more recent this story, the more effective it will be.

Share from your own life a story of how God enabled you to love a person that you didn't like.

Prayer (5 minutes)

Lead the group in prayer for God's forgiveness for rejecting others, and ask for His power to love others who are not our best friends nor in "our" group. You may want to leave time for conversational prayer, but if students start mentioning rejected students by name, it's time to close!

Option for Further Study

Though there are some difficulties in targeting outreach to the students who are social rejects in your students' world, you might try a special outreach to students who are handicapped in a physical way. Such a welcome should be preceded by a little teaching from a doctor, nurse, or social worker who can educate the group as to the special needs of these students. Then invite handicapped students and carry on your youth group activities as usual with efforts made at being inclusive but not condescending to your guests.

Additional Resources

Ideas for Social Action (Tony Campolo, Youth Specialties)
This book contains some good ideas for involving young people in practical outreach to others.

Joni (Joni Eareckson, World Wide Publications)
Offers some helpful insights on the way a rejected person feels about herself.

STRATEGY FOR OUTREACH

PERSONAL EVANGELISM   JOHN 3

SESSION 4

GET TO THE POINT!

HOW CAN I BRING CONVERSATIONS AROUND TO CHRIST?

KEY CONCEPT — Being a witness is not merely a matter of lifestyle, but it also means explaining the Gospel verbally.

GOAL — This session introduces the basic elements of the Gospel with the intent of challenging students to share it with friends.

OVERVIEW — Many people feel obligated to witness, but they have no idea how to direct conversations around to the subject of the Gospel. Even when they do, they often do not know what to say. Thus "witnessing" becomes an all-purpose word that could refer to inviting a friend to church or delivering a "hellfire and brimstone" sermon. Students must understand what the Gospel is and how to share it effectively if they are to have a verbal witness. This session gives them opportunity to start.

TIME REQUIRED — 50-55 minutes

MATERIALS CHECKLIST —
Materials needed for the basic session:
___ Bible
___ Pens
___ Prepared form *(Figuring the Fear Factor)*
___ *Four Spiritual Laws* booklet

Materials needed for optional activities:
___ Chalkboard and chalk (to record feedback)
___ Sample surveys for use at school

JUNIOR HIGH ADAPTATION — The junior higher may never have tried any type of witnessing, so you may need to modify the *Figuring the Fear Factor* activity to be a little more hypothetical, saying, "Let's suppose I were to ask you to witness; how would you feel?" Do not assume, however, that junior highers are not motivated or capable of witnessing. They may be more responsive than senior highers, and by getting them witnessing in their early teens, you can help develop habit patterns they can take through high school.

| TIPS FOR LEADERS | SESSION OUTLINE |

WARM-UP

Optional Openers (choose one)

How Not to Do It (10 minutes)

Many students think only of the bizarre methods of witnessing as options for school outreach. In this first opener, have students feed back to you the ways that they consider weird or unusual for witnessing. (You may need to generate ideas by relaying some story you have heard about people using huge Bibles, sandwich boards, or "hellfire and brimstone" sermons to witness.)

You can increase the effectiveness of this opener by coming into the meeting carrying a huge Bible or by being covered with evangelistic buttons or even bumper stickers.

Evaluation (Discussion Starters) (10 minutes)

Ask students to offer their feelings about the relative effectiveness of being witnesses for Christ using these contemporary techniques (you can add methodologies that are used in your area):

- Crusades or big meetings
- Christian musicians addressing secular audiences (like Amy Grant or Stryper)
- Holding up verse references at athletic events
- Television or radio evangelists
- Putting verses or Christian truths on a billboard
- Sending Bibles or Gospel tracts to people's homes

Remember to emphasize that you want them to evaluate the effectiveness of these techniques with their friends. The point is not to develop a critical spirit in the youth for others' methodologies.

Figuring the Fear Factor (10 minutes)

Hand out a prepared sheet (below) with a list of reasons why people are afraid to speak up about Christ. Have students rate on a scale of 1 to 7 the things that make them most afraid (1) to least afraid (7) to witness about Christ. (A variation on this is to have students or adult leaders present a skit in which a person is out trying to witness and he or she encounters *all* of the problems listed.)

Figuring the Fear Factor

Rate on a scale of 1 to 7 the things that make you most afraid (1) to least afraid (7) to witness about Christ.

____ I'm afraid that I'll ruin my reputation at school, and I'll be called a religious fanatic.
____ I'm afraid I won't know what to say.
____ I'm afraid I'll say the wrong thing and confuse the person more than help him.
____ I'm afraid that after I witness I'll do something which discredits my witness.
____ I'm afraid that if the person wants to receive Christ, I won't know what to do.
____ I'm afraid that questions about the Bible or evolution or the pagans in Asia will stump me.
____ I'm afraid the person will be a member of a cult group and try to convert me.

(If students do not put their names on these forms, they may be willing to pass their responses in. Reading these responses will help you decide where the greatest needs are in terms of training and motivating your students to witness.)

WORKOUT

Read and Discuss (15-20 minutes)

Have a student read the following passages and then discuss them in your group. The first question in each set is designed to focus on the text, and the second one should

SESSION OUTLINE

bring the text to apply to the real-life experiences of your group members.

1. John 3:1-2
Why do you think Nicodemus came to Jesus by night? (Since he was a religious leader [a Pharisee], he probably did not want anyone to know of his religious *interest* or his desire to talk to the controversial Jesus of Nazareth.)

Are there people you know who would be ashamed to admit it if they wanted to know more about Jesus? If yes, why would they be ashamed? (Athletes, popular students, etc., would often be ashamed because they would fear losing their reputation or popularity.)

2. John 3:3
Jesus got right to the point. Why did He seem to pounce on Nicodemus right away? (We don't really know, but it may be because Nicodemus' words in 3:2 sounded to Jesus like superficial flattery, and He was concerned about the deeper issues.)

What do you think are the relative pros and cons of getting right to the point when you talk with your friends? (Though asking questions like, "Are you saved?" or "Do you have a personal relationship with Christ?" may be abrupt and sometimes insensitive, there are times when these questions are the only ways to get started.)

3. John 3:4-8
What does Jesus say it means to be "born again"? (It means being spiritually born by the Holy Spirit.)

Why is it hard to use a phrase like "born again" today? If you can't say "born again," what is a better term? (The term is tough to use because it has been so popularized that we have everything from "born again" musicians whose lives give no evidence of God at work to "born again" houses with new paint jobs. Better phrases may be "converted," "become a Christian," or "committed your life to Christ.")

4. John 3:16-21
What are the basic elements of the Gospel message? (God loves us; He sent His Son; we must believe in Him as the substitute for our penalty (see verses 14-15); not to believe in Him is to love darkness and be condemned before God.)

How can you present this to your friends? (A simple presentation of belief in Jesus is the best solution, but you should listen to your students' ideas and answers.)

WRAP-UP

Role Play (10 minutes)

Ask a student to join you up front, and then explain that you are going to simulate a witnessing experience using a witnessing tool like the *Four Spiritual Laws* (or some equivalent booklet).

Go right through the booklet until the point of decision, and stop there. Doing this correctly (eye contact, staying to the booklet without getting off track, being personable, etc.) is an excellent way to show students how it can be done.

TIPS FOR LEADERS

An example out of your own life about a time you were ashamed to express your faith (like saying grace at a restaurant or reading your Bible in front of friends) can help students get started in discussion here.

A more detailed explanation of being "born again" may be useful here, though it is covered in the *Wrap-up*.

Arrange for your student partner before the meeting, and instruct him to be receptive throughout the presentation. Make sure he does not bring up every confusing question he can think of as you go through the booklet.

You may want to hand out samples of the booklet being used to encourage students to try to share it with a friend.

Summary (5 minutes)

Say: **The example of Jesus with Nicodemus shows us some good pointers about witnessing. If we are to be effective as witnesses, we too should know what we are going to say *before* we get into a witnessing situation. For that reason, having a memorized outline of the Gospel or a witnessing tool like the *Four Spiritual Laws* is useful because:**
1. **It helps us get to and stay on the main points.**
2. **It gives us greater confidence because we are no longer afraid of leaving something out.**
3. **It helps us explain the Gospel in manageable terms that friends can understand.**
4. **It brings people to a point of decision when we ask, "Would you like to put your faith in Jesus?"**

Options for Further Study

Option 1—This session is a great way of introducing a witnessing training program. If you want to respond to the *Figuring the Fear Factor* exercise, you may want to tell students that participating in the witnessing training program is the best way to alleviate their fears.

Option 2—In spite of the direction of this session to "get to the point," many students will still be asking, "How can I get into a discussion about spiritual matters?" One idea is to direct conversation to spiritual matters using a simple survey with questions like these:
1. What motivates you?
2. What do you think is worth living for?
3. What do you look forward to in the future?
4. What are your worst fears about life?

If you go the survey route, make sure to instruct your students on how to make the transition from the final question to a presentation of the Gospel.

Additional Resources

Youth Evangelism Explosion (c/o Coral Ridge Presbyterian Church, Fort Lauderdale, Florida)
This is a 15-week training program designed for use with teenagers. It is a modification of the adult Evangelism Explosion program created by Dr. James Kennedy.

Winning Ways (Leroy Eims, Victor Books)
An inspirational resource on witnessing as a way of life.

I Hate Witnessing (Rick Innes, Gospel Light)
Focuses on the honest hesitation that most will have about witnessing and offers some creative alternatives.

The Master Plan of Evangelism (Robert Coleman, Revell)
One of the best books available on the evangelistic and discipleship patterns of Jesus.

Music Box (White Lion)
A funny movie about the need to speak up about the Good News.

How to Give Away Your Faith (Paul Little, InterVarsity Press)
A basic tool for training others in evangelism.

SECTION 2

INTO THE NEIGHBORHOOD

The "world" of the typical teenager consists of a small circle of friends with whom he is very close and a larger circle (youth group, band, clubs, etc.) to which he and his friends belong. As a result, the average junior or senior higher has not learned to go beyond the boundaries of his or her world to touch the lives of others.

Getting young people to be unselfish and benevolent is no easy task, but it can be done. The four sessions in this section are designed to provide some of the cognitive foundations (for example, the knowledge that Jesus is with us) as well as the experiential foundations (actual interaction with elderly people) for service to others.

The promise of Jesus to be with us always (session 5) provides the foundation for sessions which focus on neighborhood, community, and the elderly, but these are not complete by themselves. The *experience* of serving is essential in these studies to make sure that your young people are putting action behind their beliefs.

Thus, section 2 will require some advance planning on your part. Perhaps you will want to initiate neighborhood Bible studies or community service projects to follow up on sessions 6 and 8. You could arrange to do a service project at a nursing home or start up an "Adopt-a-Granny" program to encourage practical response to session 7.

The ideal, of course, is to channel the students' energies in response to these sessions so that they—not you—are planning for neighborhood outreach.

Make sure to read over all four sessions before you start this section so that you can plan, prepare, and pray for your group to get involved in active outreach.

INTO THE NEIGHBORHOOD

OUTREACH AT SCHOOL   HEBREWS 13:5

SESSION 5

SHARING MY LOCKER WITH JESUS

CAN JESUS GO TO SCHOOL WITH ME?

KEY CONCEPT | Jesus is with us always in the midst of our outreach efforts.

GOAL | This session reminds young people that in the midst of their fears regarding outreach, Jesus is still with them.

OVERVIEW | Even students who profess faith in Christ can find it difficult to believe that Jesus understands their worlds and the tensions they face at school each day. This session focuses on the fact that Jesus is indeed with us at all times, and we can draw on His power as we seek to touch other people with His love. Knowing that He is always with us gives us the ability to overcome our fears.

TIME REQUIRED | 45-65 minutes

MATERIALS CHECKLIST | Materials needed for basic session:
___ Bible
___ Pens
___ Obstacles (*Blind Walk*)
___ Response handout (*In His Steps*)

Materials needed for optional activities:
___ Four-foot table or platform (*Trust Fall*)

JUNIOR HIGH ADAPTATION | The session is readily transferable to junior highers, but you must make sure that the "catchers" on the *Trust Fall* activity are strong enough to catch the person falling. You may want to insert a leader or older student to help out. *In His Steps* may need some modification for junior highers as well.

TIPS FOR LEADERS

SESSION OUTLINE

WARM-UP

Optional Openers (choose one or both)

Trust Fall (10 minutes)

This activity is designed to help students understand that Jesus is there, even when we cannot see Him. One student stands on a table or platform about four feet off the ground. He stands with his back to a group of six to eight people whose arms are stretched out and interlocked. These students stand in the direct line of a fall backward so that they will equally share the weight of the fall. With words of encouragement like, "You can trust us," or, "We're here," the catchers urge the person on the platform to tip backward and fall into their arms. The person falls backward and is caught by the group.

Make sure that your stronger students are distributed throughout the catchers. Also, instruct those who are falling to keep their legs straight and their arms by their side.

Neighbor Nudge (5 minutes)

Ask students to turn to neighbors behind them and beside them and respond to this question: "How would your day have been different today if Jesus had been actually (physically) with you throughout the day?"

The leader should instruct the group to change neighbors every 60 seconds or so.

Blind Walk (10-15 minutes)

Set up a short obstacle course in your meeting room using chairs, tables, etc. As you are doing this, ask students to get into groups of two. In these pairs, one person volunteers to be blindfolded and the other is the guide. Then, one pair at a time, students go together through the obstacle course. The blindfolded student must go through with his guide, but the two must never touch. The guide has to describe the path, the obstacles, and the turns that need to be made.

To get the first blindfolded person to volunteer may not be easy, so you could say, "The person whose birthday is closest to today should be blindfolded first."

After the first time through, have students change roles and go through it again. Then have them sit together in pairs for three or four minutes to discuss how they felt being dependent on someone else's voice and guidance.

At the end of this exercise (or all of the exercises), say: **It is a great challenge to understand what it means to follow the guidance of the Lord day-to-day. Yet to know that He is with us to guide us and give us power is essential if we are to be effective as witnesses for Him.**

WORKOUT

Bible Study (15-20 minutes)

Have different students read three passages: Hebrews 13:5; Matthew 28:19-20; and Romans 8:38-39; then discuss them in reverse order.

Ask students before the meeting to be your readers so they can go over the texts. The passage in Romans has some tricky words.

1. Romans 8:38-39
What are the external factors which will never be able to separate us from God and His love? (Death, life, angels, human powers, current and future events, distance, anything in creation.)

Why do you think these words would have helped the Christians at Rome? (They were afraid of death, the Roman powers of government, the future.)

To get students to go deeper than a pat answer such as "He always loves us," you may want to devise a follow-up question.

What does this say to you and me about God's love for us in the midst of changing circumstances? (His love is always present.)

2. Matthew 28:19-20
What are Jesus' disciples commanded to do? (Go to all the world and teach and baptize people as His followers.)

What promise does Jesus tack on at the end of His command? (He will be with us always.)

Why do you think such a promise would be important to His disciples? (They might have been afraid to carry out His command on their own.)

What does this promise mean to you as you try to follow Jesus?

3. Hebrews 13:5
What fears do the Hebrews seem to have which prompted the writer to quote Jesus' promise to be with them always? (According to verse 5, it seems that they may have feared loss of money, and therefore security, so they were going after it too much. The writer tells them not to love money and not to worry about it, because Jesus has promised to be with them—and therefore provide for them.)

What fears do you have about following Jesus and being a witness for Him? (Discuss answers.) **What does His promise mean for you?**

Talk-to (1 minute)

Say: **We all have a variety of fears, especially related to following Jesus' commands to "go" and reach out to others. His commands, however, are given with His promises to be with us at all times and never to desert us. We can have confidence as we stand up or step out for Him, that He is there to guide us, even as we guided each other through the** Blind Walk.

WRAP-UP

In His Steps (15 minutes)

Say: **Many years ago, a famous Christian book was written by Charles M. Sheldon entitled** In His Steps (Broadman). **The book was the story of a number of Christians whose lives were changed when they began making decisions after asking themselves, "What would Jesus do in this situation?"**

The idea behind the book was that Jesus is alive and He is with us—so we should try to live our lives "in His steps." This means following Him even as we followed each other through the Blind Walk.

When we realize that Jesus is alive and with us, our lives should change. Complete this "In His Steps" response sheet to decide where you need to change now that you understand more fully that Jesus "will never leave you or forsake you." (See page 28 for form.)

Prayer (1-2 minutes)

Close by having a time of silence when students can commit their decisions to the Lord privately. In closing, pray that God will make us all bold to stand up for Him because we realize that Jesus is always by our side.

Tips for Leaders:

Have a student or a coleader hand out the response sheets.

TIPS FOR LEADERS | SESSION OUTLINE

Option for Further Study

A study of Moses' response to God's call (Exodus 3–4) is another good example of the importance of knowing God's presence as we seek to fulfill the outreach or ministry to which He has called us. In spite of his fears, Moses was again and again reassured by God that he could undertake his responsibilities because God would be with him.

Additional Resources

Greatest Story Never Told and *Super Christian* (both films from John Schmidt Productions)
A good challenge to students regarding witnessing. The theme of depending on Jesus' power and presence is part of these films.

In His Steps

Complete by selecting your top three areas needing change.

Because I realize that Jesus is always with me . . .

___ I need to reform my language.
___ I can be more bold in telling others about Him.
___ I should stand up for my faith.
___ I can decide to go against my friends when they make decisions that displease God.
___ I should stop talking behind people's backs.
___ I can start praying more and talking to Jesus throughout the day.
___ I have a few "secret areas" of my life that I need to change so that I can please Him.
___ Other:

Encourage students to keep their responses confidential and to take them home after the meeting.

INTO THE NEIGHBORHOOD

OUTREACH IN THE NEIGHBORHOOD SELECTED PASSAGES

SESSION 6

I'LL GO ANYWHERE—BUT NEXT DOOR

HOW CAN I WITNESS TO MY NEIGHBOR?

KEY CONCEPT

The people right around us are our first, God-given responsibilities for outreach.

GOAL

This session calls young people to start caring about their neighbors through prayer and action.

OVERVIEW

Though our neighbors are geographically closest to us, they are often the hardest people to reach out to because they know us. They have seen the way we really live, and they may even know our failures and weaknesses as Christians. Starting from where we are as sinners, this session encourages some practical steps to make caring for neighbors a priority for students (and their families).

TIME REQUIRED

40–50 minutes

MATERIALS CHECKLIST

Materials required for basic session:
___ Bibles
___ Prizes (for group that wins *Scripture Search*)
___ Pens and paper

Materials needed for optional activities:
___ Prize (*Know Your Neighbors*)

JUNIOR HIGH ADAPTATION

The concepts of this session should transfer to your junior highers, but getting them to put the session into practice will be difficult. With this in mind, the option for further study (an all-group neighborhood outreach) is especially helpful in building the junior highers' confidence and understanding of how they can be "lights" in their neighborhoods.

TIPS FOR LEADERS

SESSION OUTLINE

WARM-UP

Optional Openers (choose one or both)

Know Your Neighbors (10 minutes)

Pass out a blank piece of paper and tell group members they have five minutes to list every person that they know by name who lives within an estimated two tenths of a mile of their home. After the time is up, instruct them to tally the score (10 points per person), and give a prize for the highest score.

Tell students to list each member of each family whom they know.

Acrostic (10 minutes)

Form groups of two or three and give each group a sheet of paper on which they should write the word "Neighbor" down the left-hand column. Then give the groups five to eight minutes to do one of two things. They can do words associated with neighbors (example one), or they can try to construct an actual sentence out of words beginning with the letters of "neighbor" (example two).

Showing or reading an example is helpful as long as students do not copy your example.

Example one:
Nice
Evangelize
Informal
Good works
Home
Backyard
Openness
Reach out

Example two:
Neglecting
Evangelism
Into
Geographically close
Homes
Belittles
Our
Reaching out

Wish List (5 minutes)

On a half-sheet of paper, have students write as many ideas as possible of ways that they wish their neighbors would serve them. Instruct them that "the sky is the limit," and they can list anything from "mowing my lawn" to "washing the car" to "painting the house."

You may want to close this section by reading Mark 10:45 or Matthew 20:28.

After hearing some answers, say: **We all would like to be served, but if we are to reach our neighbors with the love of Christ, we must focus our attention on serving rather than being served.**

WORKOUT

Scripture Search (15 minutes)

Using a "Bible-drill" format, instruct students to get into groups of three to four (different than the acrostic groups) with at least two Bibles.

Putting leaders with the less-motivated groups can help them stay in the competition.

Then give these instructions: **We want to look at what the Bible says about being witnesses to our neighbors, and we are going to do this in a competitive format. I will give a Bible reference, and then your team can gain points based on three areas:**
1. **the first team to have someone stand and read the verse;**
2. **the first team to answer the question I give about the verse;**
3. **the first team to determine if the verse is a "G" (general principle) verse or "S" (specific instruction) verse regarding being a witness as a neighbor.**

SESSION OUTLINE

- Galatians 6:9
  What should we *not* do as we do good works? (Grow weary.)
  "G" verse
- Proverbs 12:26 (NASB)
  What does the righteous person do for his neighbor? (Guides him.)
  "S" verse
- Matthew 5:16
  What is the purpose of good works? (For people to glorify God.)
  "G" verse
- Ephesians 2:8–10
  What is the purpose for which Christians are saved? (To do good works.)
  "G" verse
- 1 Timothy 2:1–2
  What is a good thing we can do for everyone? (Pray.)
  "G" verse
- Proverbs 14:21
  What do you do when you despise your neighbor? (Sin.)
  "S" verse
- 2 Corinthians 9:8
  When does God help us do good works? (Always.)
  "G" verse
- Matthew 22:39
  How are we to love our neighbors? (As ourselves.)
  "S" verse

Talk-to (5 minutes)

Say: **The Bible is full of verses which generally and specifically teach us to love and serve our neighbors. Let's look back at Matthew 5:16.** (Reread this verse.)

A light is brightest when it is closest to us. (You can illustrate this by shutting off the lights and using a candle. If you stand within a few feet of the group, they may get enough light to read their Bibles, but as you move away, their ability to see the print decreases.) **Jesus says that we are supposed to be lights, and we are to let our lights shine. The "light" of Jesus' love that we project should be brightest around the people that we are closest to—our neighbors.**

Many of us, however, prefer to ignore our neighbors. We may not like them, or they may have done something years ago that has created a little "feud" between us and them.

Nevertheless, our light should be brightest around the people we live near, so we must make attempts to be lights to our neighbors. Here are a few simple ideas:

1. **Good works—"let us not lose heart in doing good" (Galatians 6:9, NASB). Choose something that you think your neighbors would appreciate, and do it.**
2. **Prayer—"I urge that prayers . . . be made on behalf of all men" (1 Timothy 2:1, NASB). Find out your neighbors' names and start praying for them.**
3. **Sharing—"The righteous is a guide to his neighbor" (Proverbs 12:26, NASB). As you build new friendships, make sure to share your love for Christ with your neighbor, both through your activities and your words.**

TIPS FOR LEADERS

Make sure to prepare a coleader or student to control the room's lighting.

TIPS FOR LEADERS | SESSION OUTLINE

WRAP-UP

Bridging the Neighbor GAP (5 minutes)

Say: **On a blank sheet of paper, write the three letters G-A-P vertically down the left column, and leave space to write things on the right.**

Start by thinking of a neighbor—it can be someone your age or someone else—that you would like to start reaching out to. Write that person's name on your page.

Now concerning that person, think of three things that you can start doing in these areas, and write them to the side of your G-A-P.

1. *Good works*—a specific kind act that you are going to do for your neighbor in the next week (remember the way you wanted to be served in your "Wish List").
2. *Affirmation*—something special that you will do in the next two or three weeks to make that neighbor feel special (invite him to your home, bring him a snack, etc.).
3. *Prayer*—can you commit yourself to praying for that neighbor every day for the next month? (If you keep on praying for that person, God will show you new ways to reach out and care.)

You can close the meeting in prayer after each person has filled in the G-A-P on his or her sheet of paper.

Option for Further Study

An all-group outreach to a person who is a neighbor to the church is an excellent way to put this session into practice. By applying the G-A-P exercise to that person, you can show the students how it is done and encourage students to do the same in their own neighborhoods.

Additional Resources

Ideas for Social Action (Tony Campolo, Youth Specialties)
Offers some good suggestions on neighborhood and community service projects.

Out of the Salt Shaker and Into the World (Rebecca Manley Pippert, InterVarsity Press)
A useful text for leaders to help them get a vision for lifestyle evangelism.

Tips for Leaders sidebar:

Rather than relying on blank sheets of paper, you may want to prepare a G-A-P printed handout in advance.

Reporting at the next meeting on personal progress is essential.

INTO THE NEIGHBORHOOD

OUTREACH TO THE ELDERLY SELECTED PASSAGES

SESSION 7

TAKING GOLD TO THE GOLDEN-AGERS

DO OLD PEOPLE REALLY NEED ME?

KEY CONCEPT | Effective outreach includes caring for old people.

GOAL | This session introduces the challenge of caring for and serving the elderly of the community.

OVERVIEW | Stereotypes, bad experiences, and actual separation from old people can keep teenagers from reaching out to the aged, yet these are often the most responsive and needy people in the community. By seeing elderly people from God's perspective and by breaking down some of the barriers that exist between young and old, this session builds the foundation for potential long-term outreach to and relationships with the elderly.

TIME REQUIRED | 45-65 minutes

MATERIALS CHECKLIST | Materials needed for basic session:
___ Bibles
___ Pens
___ Church letterhead (*You May Feel Old But....*)

Materials needed for optional activities:
___ Pens and paper
___ "Adoption" program sign-up list

JUNIOR HIGH ADAPTATION | It may be easier to get junior highers involved in caring for the elderly because young teens are often more enthusiastic and less inhibited. However, they need more instruction on caring for these people because naiveté can become insensitivity if not monitored. In this session, the optional openers (*Wisdom Collection* and *The Favorite Story*) may not work well with junior highers who have not been with elderly people very much. The rest of the session should be readily transferable. Following through with caring for the elderly will work best with junior highers if you have one leader working with every four or five students.

TIPS FOR LEADERS | SESSION OUTLINE

WARM-UP

Optional Openers

Wisdom Collection (10 minutes)

In small groups, have students write down a collection of wise sayings or lessons that they have learned from the elderly people they know—grandparents, neighbors, or family friends. Then have each group share responses to form a youth group "Wisdom Collection."

"Priming the pump" with a few examples is a good idea.

The Favorite Story (10 minutes)

Just about every student knows the one or two favorite stories that his grandmother or grandfather may like to tell during every visit. Have students share some of these stories in small groups. Then discuss together why you think these stories might be so memorable or important to your grandparents.

One adult leader per small group is recommended. Make sure the adult leader has a personal story to relate.

Imagination Game (10 minutes)

This game is designed to help students try to feel the pains and fears of the elderly. Try to maintain a fairly serious attitude in the group as you go through these, for too much humor will tend to foster mockery of the elderly rather than compassion for them.

Say: **We want to try to imagine what it is like to be an elderly person. I am going to give you a phrase that describes the real world in which many older people live. Then I want you to offer your thoughts and feedback as to how you would feel if you were in their position.**

1. If my body was not functioning the way I wanted it to, I would feel . . .
2. If nobody from my family ever visited me, I would feel . . .
3. If people kept telling me I was in my "golden" years, I would feel . . .
4. If all my friends and my spouse had died, I would feel . . .
5. If I were really unsure as to where my money would come from, I would feel . . .
6. If every day I was reminded by my body that I am going to die soon, I would feel . . .
7. If I started forgetting things so much that I thought I was going crazy, I would feel . . .
8. If everything around me was changing so fast that I knew I could never keep up, I would feel . . .
9. If I went into a store and young kids laughed at me because of my looks, I would feel . . .
10. If no one ever called me on the phone, I would feel . . .

Depending on the size of your group, you may want to share these answers in small groups.

After this "game," say: **We really do not know everything about how old people think or feel, but we can understand why so many of them are fearful, lonely, and frustrated. One of the solutions to their problems is understanding how God sees them, but they can understand best that God loves them as we show love to them.**

A recent "case study" from the newspaper that illustrates how elderly people feel about themselves can help reinforce your point here.

34

SESSION OUTLINE | TIPS FOR LEADERS

WORKOUT

Group Study (15 minutes)

Start by saying: **So that we can communicate God's love and concern to the old people in our lives, we must understand God's view of them. Let's look at a variety of Bible verses related to elderly people.** Read the passages one at a time and ask the questions.

1. Proverbs 20:29
What is the difference between old men and young men? (Young men glory in physical strength, while old men are honored by gray hair.) **Why is gray hair an honor?** (The people of the Old Testament saw gray hair as a sign of wisdom that has been accumulated with a long life.)

2. Psalm 37:25
What is the old psalmist's testimony? (In all his years, God had always been faithful to His people, the "righteous.") **What can we learn from old people?** (Those that follow Christ can tell us of how God has always taken care of them.)

3. Ephesians 6:2-3 (or Exodus 20:12)
What is one of the rewards of obeying your parents? (A long life.) (Read also Proverbs 10:27.)

4. Matthew 25:35-36
What are two ways we serve the Lord by serving the elderly? (By caring for those who are lonely [the "stranger"] and by visiting the sick.) **As we care for the elderly, who are we caring for?** (The Lord wants us to act toward them the same way as we would if we were serving Him in person.)

5. James 1:27
What does God consider "true religion"? (Visiting orphans and widows and staying free from worldly sins.) **Why are orphans and widows so special to God?** (Because they are the outcasts and the lonely that He is especially concerned about.)

Close this portion of the session by reading these verses: "Is not wisdom found among the aged? Does not long life bring understanding?" (Job 12:12) "Gray hair is a crown of splendor; it is attained by a righteous life" (Proverbs 16:31).

Then say: **God considers old persons very special because their long lives have helped them accumulate wisdom. We need to see them as people not only loved by God, but blessed by God with years of experience from which we can learn.**

This can be done in small groups or in one large group, as long as a few students do not dominate the answers in the large group.

WRAP-UP

You May Feel Old But.... (15 minutes)

Based on the Scripture study of this session, have your students write a letter to elderly people at a nursing home or retirement village entitled "You May Feel Old But...."

If your group is larger than 10, break into groups of 5 or 6. Give them some church letterhead and say: **Just as you and I do, elderly people suffer from feelings of low self-esteem, thinking, "Nobody likes me" or "I wish I were dead." God's message to these people, however, is quite different. He sees them**

One leader per group is recommended.

TIPS FOR LEADERS | SESSION OUTLINE

as valuable, wise, and special. But old people do not know God's view of them unless somebody tells them, and that is what we want to do.

Using the Scriptures we looked at earlier, write a letter to the folks at _____ (choose a nursing home in your community) **nursing home. Explain to them that—as teenagers—you understand a little of the feelings they are going through, but that you want them to know what God thinks of them. Then summarize some of the lessons we learned from the Bible; you can quote verses if you like. When you are done, sign your full names. Remember to write clearly.**

Testimony (5 minutes)

There are two options here. First, you could have a group member testify of his involvement with the elderly and how it has helped produce growth in his life. Or you could have an elderly member of your church tell your group how much it means to him or her to be cared for by others.

The latter option may be desirable because it can lead into a question and answer period. Either option, however, will take some advance preparation on your part.

Options for Further Study

Option 1—A visit to or service at a nursing home or elderly housing area is especially appropriate as a response to this session. If you decide to do this, make sure to prepare the people you plan to visit (do not just "drop by"). Prepare your young people for what they may see; instruct them on how to care, to ask questions, and to listen.

If you decide to pursue an "adoption" program at the close of this session, make sure to have a sign-up sheet available.

Option 2—An "adoption" program is an effective way to give students an opportunity for ongoing relationships with and outreach to the elderly. Working cooperatively with agencies that serve the aging, you can match up interested students with an elderly man or woman to visit every week. In addition to the love this shows to the elderly people, it also provides great growth opportunities for your students, especially those that may not have grandparents in the area.

Additional Resources

Handbook on Service (Dale Dieleman, Baker)
Suggests projects that can be done in serving the elderly.

How to Help the Hurting (Everett L. Worthington, InterVarsity Press)
A resource for practical ways to let people know that you care about their loneliness and pain.

INTO THE NEIGHBORHOOD

OUTREACH IN THE COMMUNITY   SELECTED PASSAGES

SESSION 8

GOING TO TOWN WITH JESUS

HOW CAN I AFFECT MY TOWN FOR CHRIST?

KEY CONCEPT | Our Christian faith should be applied in the community in which we live.

GOAL | Students are shown the importance of being witnesses as a group and as individuals in the community.

OVERVIEW | We frequently operate our youth groups and churches with little or no regard for our community, community leaders, and the people who protect us (police and fire departments). This session starts by enlarging our vision (realizing that Christ's love applies in the town as well as at church), and then shows some practical ways to put our faith to work as we reach out in the community.

TIME REQUIRED | 50-70 minutes

MATERIALS CHECKLIST | Materials needed for basic session:
____ Bibles
____ Pens and paper *(Jesus Speaks)*
____ Chalkboard or overhead projector

JUNIOR HIGH ADAPTATION | This session is very usable with junior highers. The only adaptation might be to temper their enthusiasm as you develop ideas of serving the community. Your role should be to help them to dream while simultaneously being realistic about what can be done by a group your size.

| TIPS FOR LEADERS | SESSION OUTLINE |

WARM-UP

Optional Openers

Case Study (10 minutes)

Share the following true story about one youth group's experience of community outreach.

> The young people at Grace Church are about to go caroling; Christmas is only two weeks away. As the group comes together for the weekly meeting, the leader tries to generate some enthusiasm, but it is obvious that no one is too excited.
>
> Excitement builds, however, as the leader asks, "Do you think we should go caroling in downtown Lexington or downtown Bedford?" About half the group is from Lexington and the other half from Bedford. The leader is glad about the enthusiasm, and he thinks, *Each student wants to make sure we go to his town.*
>
> The facts, however, are different. As a vote is taken, students reveal that each one wants to go to the neighboring town, not his own. One girl actually says, "If I went downtown and my friends saw me, I think I would die."

Discussion Questions

You may want to record these answers on the chalkboard for discussion purposes.

1. **Why would students prefer not to go caroling in their own town?**

2. **What is so bad about being seen witnessing (even in a mild way like caroling) in your own town?**

3. **If you were put in this position, which option would you prefer (your own town or a neighboring town)?**

4. **If you were the leader, what would you do?** (In the real situation the leader took the students to both towns.)

Feedback (5 minutes)

Have someone save this list of suggestions to be used as part of the Brainstorm later in the session.

Using a chalkboard or overhead projector to record answers, ask your youth group: **What needs are there in our community that we could act together to meet as a witness to God's love in our lives?** (As students offer answers, try to get a feel for which ideas really would work so that you could potentially follow this session with a community outreach project.)

Jesus Speaks (15 minutes)

Reading a sample speech might be helpful.

Instruct the youth group that Jesus is coming to your community (at least in your minds, at this meeting). In groups of three or four, have members make up a little introductory speech that Jesus would give (as you imagine it) if He came to your community to address the following groups:

1. Police
2. Firemen
3. Government officials
4. Local clergy and religious leaders
5. Country club members

38

SESSION OUTLINE | TIPS FOR LEADERS

    6. Community merchants and store owners
    7. Local teachers
    8. Health care workers
    9. Public works department
   10. Owners of the community newspaper

After you hear responses, say: **We don't often think about the fact that Jesus wants to come to our community and speak to the people who affect our lives here, but He does! Jesus does have something to say to these people, but He wants to say it through us, and we are His spokesmen. For this reason, we want to look at the way that God calls us to reach our community.**

WORKOUT

Discussion Group (15-20 minutes)

Introduce this session's Bible study by saying: **In your groups, we are going to look at several passages which offer some instructions or examples about what it means to be witnesses in our community. After you read the suggested passage, discuss together: "What do these verses tell us about reaching out to our own towns or cities?"** (Note: several of these passages have been used in earlier sessions, so students should be familiar with them.)

   Group 1—Mark 5:1-20 (The passage shows that one man, who had an exceptional testimony, was used to reach his own community [Decapolis] even though he preferred traveling with Jesus.)

   Group 2—Matthew 8:28-34 (A similar passage, only this one shows that our reaching out to our community will not always be welcome. When Jesus healed these demoniacs, He caused such an uproar that people asked Him to leave town.)

   Group 3—Matthew 5:14-16 (Being "lights" to our community is part of following Christ, but your group should discuss what this means for your situation.)

   Group 4—Jonah 3:1-10 (When we do reach out to bring God's Word to others, He will use it to bring about changes [repentance] in their lives.)

   Group 5—Micah 6:8 and Deuteronomy 10:12 (The commands of the Lord to do justice and to love kindness can be applied to our community outreach. Make sure to ask students what these terms should mean for *you*.)

Tip: One leader per group is ideal.

Summary (5 minutes)

Say: **Concerning our outreach to our community, the Bible is clear on several points:**

1. **We are supposed to be "light" to others, showing them the love of Christ through good works.**
2. **We need to focus our attention at home. We need to realize that God does not call each of us overseas or out of our communities.**
3. **We need to preach God's Word and allow Him to lead people to respond either positively (as they did with Jonah) or negatively (as they did after Jesus healed the two demoniacs).**

TIPS FOR LEADERS

Sharing an example of another youth group's efforts at community outreach can help your group understand that they can do it (see *Additional Resources*).

SESSION OUTLINE

WRAP-UP

Brainstorm (10 minutes)

Using a chalkboard or overhead transparency, record students' feedback to this exercise. Suggest a community outreach—like visiting people in the hospital, raking the city hall lawn, etc.—and then have students suggest what they think are the obstacles and the opportunities of such a project.

Example: Spend a day doing trash pick-up around town.

Obstacles: Transportation; need for trash bags; not enough students to do a good job; we might fail; our friends might laugh at us.

Opportunities: It's a great service to the town; it might be covered by the local paper; we could tell people we're doing it because we love Jesus; we could change people's stereotypes about teenagers.

Confession (5 minutes)

Say: **To close our session tonight, let's get quiet before God and admit to Him that sometimes we just don't care that much about our town. Sometimes we don't care whether Jesus speaks to our community or not. Let's admit to Jesus our lack of love and then ask Him to give us a love for people where we live. After a few minutes of silence, I will close in prayer.**

Options for Further Study

Option 1—Police departments often have people who are willing to come speak to youth groups about the needs and opportunities for youth groups to be involved in serving the community. You may want to follow up this session with a policeman as a guest speaker. (This is also a good way to show students how to pray specifically for leaders of your city or town.)

Option 2—A Bible study of Matthew 5:13-16 with the response question, "How can we be salt and light in our town?" is a good, practical follow-up to this session.

Option 3—Going to town or city offices can be educational for your group, and you will usually find public officials very willing to visit with and answer the questions of your youth group. Plan ahead, though, to ensure the best experience.

Additional Resources

How to Build a Youth Outreach Ministry (Bill Stearns, Victor Books)
Has some excellent suggestions on how to develop student interest in service projects.

Ideas for Social Action (Tony Campolo, Youth Specialties)
Very useful in suggesting ideas for reaching out in the community.

SECTION 3

BEHIND THE BARRIERS

Of all the inner emotions that motivate teenagers, fear is certainly high on the list. Fear of the unknown, fear of failure, and fear of getting hurt all play a part when young people consider outreach to people who are "different."

The four sessions of this section are designed to help students overcome some of these fears. It is important for you to reassure your students that these fears are all normal and it is OK to have them, but they should not be controlled by such fears.

Section 3 is built on the first two sections and should be used after some of these truths have been well-established. Reminding your young people of God's view of people (session 1) and of Jesus' ongoing presence (session 5) is a good way to introduce this new section.

In the planning of these sessions, remember to be growing alongside of your young people. Identifying your own fears about people who are "different" and responding to these fears by crossing your own cultural, ethnic, or social barriers will help you set an excellent example.

Another way to increase the effectiveness of these sessions is to develop a "sister" relationship with a youth group that is culturally, ethnically, or economically different than yours. This can help students practice the truths they are learning.

Don't be surprised if you begin to get some opposition to these sessions. Even parents (who can also be very fearful of people who are "different") may oppose the idea of outreach to people they don't understand. To reduce such opposition:
- Make your focus the Bible and not your own opinions or someone else's stereotypes.
- Advise parents *in advance* of what you're doing so they can keep students home if they are in disagreement with your plans.
- Share your plans with church leaders so they will be behind you.

As you start section 3, fasten your seat belt. The truths that are explored and the stereotypes that are challenged can cause some serious discomfort for you, your young people, and maybe even your church. But no one ever said that following Jesus was easy!

BEHIND THE BARRIERS

ACROSS ETHNIC BARRIERS   SELECTED PASSAGES

SESSION 9

I'M OK, BUT WHAT ABOUT YOU?

HOW CAN I REACH OUT TO PEOPLE
WHO ARE DIFFERENT THAN I?

KEY CONCEPT — We are all scared to reach out to people we do not fully understand or identify with.

GOAL — This session is designed to help students start building bridges to those outside of their ethnic group.

OVERVIEW — Prejudice, racism, and bigotry are all enemies to the Gospel and deter us from sharing the love of Christ with sincerity and effectiveness. This session identifies the prejudices that we all have and then shows how we can win over them and actually reach out to people from different ethnic groups and backgrounds.

TIME REQUIRED — 45-60 minutes

MATERIALS CHECKLIST

Materials needed for basic session:
____ Paper, markers *(Advertisement Brochure* and *Traffic Signs)*
____ Old magazines *(Advertisement Brochure)*, scissors, and tape or glue
____ Bibles
____ Can and questions *(Can of Questions)*

Materials needed for optional activities:
____ Handout or overhead transparency *(Respond)*

JUNIOR HIGH ADAPTATION — Using this session with junior highers should be relatively easy. You may want to forgo the optional *Panel Discussion* unless your speakers can answer the questions in terms that are clearly understandable and interesting to junior highers. The optional *Respond* activity is also best left out as it may require them to respond to statements they really do not understand.

TIPS FOR LEADERS | SESSION OUTLINE

WARM-UP

Optional Openers

Respond (5 minutes)

It is often observed that 20th-century America has a very white, middle-class view of Jesus and God. It helps students to identify their own ideas. You can start them thinking by asking them to respond to these statements:
- "We in the Christian church are too often guilty of fostering the image of a white, middle-class God."
- "Jesus was a white man."
- "God shows special favor to the United States."
- "The *normal* way to worship God is the way we do it at our church."
- "If Jesus walked the earth today, He would feel right at home at our church."

You should modify these statements according to stereotypes or misconceptions that are held in your group according to their social, economic, and ethnic base.

The key here is to try to find out how much your students link Christianity with the United States.

Panel Discussion (15 minutes)

From your church or youth group, ask four or five adults or young people who come from ethnically identified groups (Hispanic, black, Jewish, Polish, Oriental, etc.) to take part in a panel discussion. Start the discussion with two or three questions of your own (samples below), and then open it up for the group to ask questions.

You might begin with these questions:
1. How strongly linked do you feel to your ethnic heritage?
2. What do you feel like when your ethnic group is the topic of someone else's joke?
3. Do you feel that people at church are sensitive to your ethnic background?
4. Does your ethnic background affect at all the way you perceive God or relate to Him?
5. How else does prejudice against your ethnic heritage manifest itself?

If you use adults, brief them beforehand so that their answers are geared to your group members.

Encourage panel members to be honest and to offer suggestions as to how the church could be more sensitive.

Advertisement Brochure (15 minutes)

Start by saying: **We all believe that the church is supposed to be a place where anyone, from any ethnic group or background, will feel welcome to experience the love of Christ. Nevertheless, people who are different often do not feel welcome.** (Hand out paper, markers, old magazines, and tape or glue.)

In your groups, it is your job to design a brochure which will help people feel welcome at church. Use Scripture verses, pictures of people from various ethnic groups, and popular slogans ("Come One, Come All," "You're Number One," etc.) to create a brochure which will create greater ethnic diversity in your church.

After this exercise, have students show their brochures. If there is still time, use them to discuss reasons why people of ethnic minorities might not feel welcome at your church.

A sample brochure and some potential verses will help students understand what you are looking for.

SESSION OUTLINE | TIPS FOR LEADERS

●WORKOUT

Can of Questions (15-20 minutes)

Many Scriptures, especially on the life of Jesus, demonstrate God's love for people outside of the normal ethnic or social group. To encourage students to listen to all of the following texts, tell them that after the Scriptures are read, a can will circulate containing questions they will be asked to answer.

Texts to be read:
1. Galatians 3:28
2. Luke 10:29-37
3. Matthew 5:38-47
4. Luke 17:11-19
5. 2 Kings 5:1-14

Encourage students to do the reading.

These are some of the questions that you should include:
From Galatians 3:28:
1. Do all ethnic groups disappear in Christ?
2. Is everyone equal in Christ? Why?
3. Does the Bible say that sexual differences or social distinctions should be abolished?

You may want to explain the intense ethnic significance of being Gentile or Samaritan to the Jewish readers of the New Testament.

From Luke 10:29-37:
4. Why does Jesus tell the story of the Good Samaritan?
5. Did the priest, Levite, or Samaritan know the man who got robbed?
6. What does Jesus teach is the way we should treat "neighbors" whom we do not know or who might be ethnically different from us?

From Matthew 5:38-47:
7. If someone from an ethnic minority has hurt us, how should we respond?
8. If I consider a person my enemy, or my group an enemy to another group, how should I act as a Christian?
9. Why should we love our enemies?

From Luke 17:11-19:
10. Why did the 10 sick men stand at a distance to Jesus?
11. What happens to the 10 lepers?
12. What is the significance of the ethnic identification of the one healed leper who returned to thank Jesus?

From 2 Kings 5:1-14:
13. Why was the king of Israel upset at the letter from the king of Syria?
14. What ethnic prejudices does Naaman demonstrate when Elisha gives the command?
15. Why is the story of Naaman a story of God's love for all people?

Remind students that Naaman is a Syrian, a people who often were at war with the Jews.

After the passages are read, have students close their Bibles. Pass the can around so that people get at least one question each (or, in the case of group studies, one question per group). Ask them to answer the question without opening the Bible. (If they do not know the answer, give them the Scripture reference on the question so they can look up the answer.)

| TIPS FOR LEADERS | SESSION OUTLINE |

WRAP-UP

Greek Study (1 minute)

Tell your group: **The words which we translate "nations" in Matthew 28:19 are *ta ethne*. What English word is directly related to the Greek word for nations?** (Ethnic.) **When we read Jesus' Great Commission, we should understand that He is concerned for every ethnic group to come to have faith in Him; this is one of our motivations for going outside of our own group to reach out to others.**

Writing ethne on the board can help students visualize it as the root of ethnic.

Talk-to (5 minutes)

Say: **According to the teaching of the Bible and the example of Jesus, Christians are supposed to be lovers of all people, regardless of ethnic group or race or color. In our sinful world, however, this is hard to do. We all have a lot of growing to do in this respect, so consider three simple steps to help your growth:**

Step One: Recognize the biblical examples. Jesus reached out to Samaritans and Gentiles—ethnic groups that His people, the Jews, would have hated. Elisha healed a Syrian; Ruth and Rahab (both Gentiles) were put by God in the line of the Messiah (Matthew 1:5); and Paul wrote that ethnic differences were to be laid aside by people who follow Christ.

Step Two: Repent of your bad attitudes. Maybe you need to ask people to forgive you for your racist or prejudiced attitudes. Perhaps you have some "enemies" that you need to start loving or praying for.

Step Three: Reach out to people who are different than you. Identify one or two people that you have stayed away from because of ethnic differences and determine to start reaching out to those people.

Traffic Signs (5 minutes)

Close the session by making traffic signs which can be put in the youth room to remind the whole group of the diversity in the body of Christ. The traffic signs should have a basic command, a Bible verse, and a short message. Use the ones below as examples.

Show a sample sign to help students understand the assignment.

Sign	Scripture	Message
GO	Matthew 28:19	Make disciples in all ethnic groups.
STOP	Galatians 3:28	Don't let differences separate you.
CAUTION	2 Kings 5:1-14	Don't let ethnic barriers get in the way of God's action.
DO NOT ENTER	Matthew 5:38-47	You can't let hatred enter your heart.

Options for Further Study

Option 1—Take your group into an ethnic neighborhood in a nearby city that is different from your group's ethnic roots. Then instruct your young people to do a study entitled "Developing a Positive Appreciation" which focuses on the positive things of the people and area you are observing. Asking students to contrast their observations with their own experience can help them appreciate the fact that some people's ethnic differences are actually better.

Examples: A. In this neighborhood, people sit out on the front steps and talk. In my neighborhood, people stay in their houses or their own yards.
B. In this neighborhood, people speak two languages. In my neighborhood, I never hear anything but English.

Option 2—Ethnic studies can be a positive learning tool for your group, especially if there is some group nearby that is ethnically different than your church. Studying the structure of families, the celebration of holidays, and even the worship of God in various ethnic traditions can be a very fruitful learning experience which can stretch your young people. (It can also yield a positive "sister-church" relationship which will build bridges.)

Additional Resources

Loving Enough to Care (Earl Wilson, Multnomah)
A good general tool in cultivating an attitude of caring toward others.

Let Justice Roll Down (John Perkins, Word)
The powerful testimony of one man's victory over hatred and the racism of others by the power of Jesus Christ.

So Long, Sweet Jesus (Bill Milliken, Zondervan)
A suburban white man's story of how he learned a new understanding of Jesus through his life and ministry in the inner city.

BEHIND THE BARRIERS

ACROSS CULTURAL BARRIERS   ACTS 10:9-48

SESSION 10

BUT WE'VE ALWAYS DONE IT THIS WAY!

HOW COME PEOPLE ARE SO DIFFERENT?

KEY CONCEPT	The fact that people are different does not mean that one is right and the other wrong.
GOAL	This session seeks to help students develop cultural appreciation and sensitivity so that they can reach out more effectively.
OVERVIEW	We all tend to think that our cultural values, holidays, ways of dressing, and ways of doing things are the right ways and that other people's values are "weird" or "strange." Understanding that it is all right to be different can help students be more culturally sensitive as they seek to witness and reach out to others. This session helps us see our normal way of thinking and then shows us how we need to modify it so that we can reach out effectively to others.
TIME REQUIRED	40-60 minutes
MATERIALS CHECKLIST	Materials needed for basic session: ____ Paper and pens ____ Bibles ____ Handout (*Bible Study*) ____ Response card (*Taking Action*) Materials needed for optional activities: ____ Handout (*True/False*) and pencils
JUNIOR HIGH ADAPTATION	This session should transfer for use with junior highers fairly easily, but you may want to revise the vocabulary in some places. You may discover that some of your students do not have sharply defined cultural values, so you may have to help them clarify their own views before you proceed to understanding the values of others.

SESSION OUTLINE | TIPS FOR LEADERS

● WARM-UP

Optional Openers

True/False (10 minutes)

Ask group members to decide if these statements are true or false, and then discuss their answers. Distribute these 10 statements on a handout.

1. ____ People in England drive on the wrong side of the road.
2. ____ December 25 is *the* day to celebrate Christmas.
3. ____ Husbands and wives should sit together at church.
4. ____ Primitive tribesmen should be taught to wear clothes.
5. ____ Church meetings should last an hour or less.
6. ____ The best way to thank people is to give a monetary gift.
7. ____ Children are too noisy for church and should be sent to another place for "junior church."
8. ____ Controlling your emotions is a sign of maturity.
9. ____ People who do not speak English are ignorant.
10. ____ Learning to read and write is basic for success.

Instruct students to record their opinions rather than being overly concerned with technicalities in the wording of the statements.

Discussion: All of these statements reflect North American cultural values and not necessarily universal values. Help your group distinguish between being *different* and being *wrong*. Here are some cultural value observations that you may want to share:

1. People in England drive on the left. There is nothing "wrong" about it. (As a matter of fact, if you think right is "right," try driving in England.)
2. Christmas is celebrated on December 25 in many parts of the world, but there is nothing inspired about that date.
3. In many cultures, men and women are on separate sides of the church when they worship.
4. Primitive tribesmen may decide to wear clothes to protect them from bugs or the sun, but the decision should be left up to them.
5. In many cultures, services run two or three or more hours, and less than this is considered insincere.
6. Some cultural groups would be insulted by payment; they would prefer a "thank you" or hospitality in return.
7. Many people keep children with them all during the worship service to teach them to be reverent.
8. In some cultures, uncontrolled crying at funerals is expected; keeping emotions under control would be considered an insult to the dead person.
9. This may be our opinion, but it's very wrong. In light of the thousands of languages in the world, we must not overestimate the importance of English.
10. This is not necessarily true in cultures that depend on farming and agriculture.

This is one of the key themes of the session, so you may want to reiterate it here: being different does not mean being wrong.

African Brainteaser (5 minutes)

Ask students to enter the culture of East Africa for a moment and try to solve a riddle:

A man has a leopard, a goat, and a basket of cassava leaves that he needs to get across the river in his boat. He can only fit one item in his boat at a time, yet he knows that the goat will eat the leaves if left with them, and the leopard will eat the goat if it is not guarded. How does he get across the river? (Answer: He takes the goat across and puts it on the other side. He returns for the cassava leaves and takes them across. On the return trip, he takes the goat back. He takes the leopard and leaves the goat. Then he returns for the goat.)

Someone is bound to ask you what a cassava is. It is a family of tropical plants with fleshy edible rootstocks which yield a nutritious starch.

49

TIPS FOR LEADERS	SESSION OUTLINE

Last Name Game (15 minutes)

Select last names that are clearly diverse in cultural background—Arabic, French, Jewish, Russian, Polish, Italian, and many other last names are quite distinctive.

This activity will take some preparation, but it helps students develop a positive appreciation for cultures and people (who may live within your community). Explain that you have selected five last names out of the local telephone directory, and they are now assigned the job of being detectives based only on the last name.

Having one leader per group that you have briefed beforehand is ideal for the success of this activity.

In groups, students are assigned the task of writing a fictitious cultural history of one of the persons that their group is assigned (or all five). Some of the things you can encourage them to include are cultural distinctives such as:
- Where did this person come from?
- What was his native language or style of dress?
- What was his native religion?
- How does he celebrate holidays (and what holidays does he celebrate)?
- What cultural distinctives does he still adhere to in this country?
- Does his cultural background affect his view of the United States?
- What brought this person (or his forefathers) to this country? Is he glad they came?

This is the most important learning section of this activity, so you may want to give students a sample of what you are looking for. (Example: Mr. Ali comes from an Islamic background, so he follows Mohammed rather than Jesus. He has never been able to forgive Christians for the slaughtering of his people during the Holy Crusades.)

Then, as detectives, encourage your students to close their reports by completing this statement: "When considering this person as a potential convert to Christianity, remember to be sensitive to these cultural factors: _____."
The answers may vary, but they should help get your group sensitized to the fact that our cultural backgrounds do affect us and the way that we think.

WORKOUT

Bible Study (15-20 minutes)

One leader per group is ideal. Help your leaders by having them preview the passage in advance.

Instruct your young people to get into groups of three or four and to read Acts 10:9-48. Hand out this list of questions which they are to try to answer. Answers in parentheses are for your use.

(Verses 9-14) **1. Why would Peter consider these animals "unclean"? See also Leviticus 11:20-25.** (Because the Law commanded against eating them.)
2. Do you think Peter thought this dream might have been a test from God? (This is certainly implied by his pious answer in verse 14.)
(Verses 15-16) **3. What is God's message to Peter?** (If God has cleansed it, don't call it unholy.)
(Verses 17-23) **4. After the vision, what does Peter do?** (He obeys God and follows His leading to Caesarea.)
(Verses 24-29) **5. What application has Peter made from his dream?** (That he should now be willing to associate with the Gentiles whom he had formerly considered unclean.)
(Verses 30-33) **6. What is the background to this encounter?** (Cornelius had had a vision too.)
(Verses 34-43) **7. What lesson does Peter learn about God?** (God does not show favoritism to people based on cultural or ethnic heritage, but He is loving to all.)
8. What lesson does Peter learn about people? (That anyone—from any nation—who fears God and obeys Him is accepted by Him.)
(Verses 44-48) **9. What is the result?** (The Holy Spirit falls on these people as well.)

Share your answers to get the whole group thinking of Peter's encounter with Cornelius, and then ask the group these two questions:
1. **What would have naturally turned Peter off to the thought of reaching out to Cornelius?** (His race, religion, eating habits, and lifestyle were all strange to Peter.)

SESSION OUTLINE | **TIPS FOR LEADERS**

2. **What is God's message to Peter and to us?** (Do not get turned off by external things; rather, focus on a person's desire to know God.)

WRAP-UP

Talk-to (5 minutes)

Say to your group: **Effectiveness as witnesses for Christ means that we must be sensitive to the people that we are trying to reach and their cultural values and practices. We learn a few things from Peter and Cornelius which we must remember:**
1. *Cultural differences can turn us off.* **The way someone looks, the music he listens to, or even the way he talks can scare us and make us unwilling to try to reach out. If we are to love people, however, we must work at overcoming this fear.**
2. *God's concern is for people's hearts.* **The external factors are not nearly as important to God as they are to us. His primary concern is to reach those people who are genuinely seeking Him.**
3. *We must obey God (as Peter did) and go to those who are different than we are.* **It is clear that being different does not mean being wrong. We should learn to overcome our cultural biases and reach out as God wants us to.**

Encourage students to make note of these three points.

Taking Action (5 minutes)

Instruct group members to think about one student (or teacher) at their school whom they think is culturally different from them. Then ask for a commitment from your students to do the following:
1. Start praying daily for that person.
2. Try to meet him or her *this week*.
3. Ask him if you could meet one-on-one for an hour to find out about his background (use some of the questions from the *Last Name Game* exercise).
4. Share about your belief in Jesus Christ as the opportunities arise.

Do some research before this session so that you are aware of the various culturally unique students at local schools. This will help you to deflect students' comments that "There are no students like this at my school."

Having a response card will help students remember that particular student or teacher.

Always keep in mind the fact that *this* is our goal. We are not just seeking to appreciate other cultures. We want to help these people understand the reality of a relationship with Jesus Christ.

Options for Further Study

Option 1—International Missions (Pequannock, New Jersey) and other mission groups offer seminars on witnessing to Muslims, Hindus, and others of culturally diverse backgrounds. They can train the group on ways to understand, appreciate, and respond to cultural values in a way that will enhance the presentation of the Gospel.

Option 2—A missionary is often an excellent resource for understanding cultural differences and how these should affect our presentation of the Gospel.

Additional Resources

Share Your Faith with a Muslim (C.F. Marsh, Moody Press)
Teaches how to understand Islam and apply the Christian Gospel to it.

Share the New Life with a Jew (Moishe and Ceil Rosen, Moody Press)
How to overcome cultural differences so that Jews can see Jesus as the Messiah.

Games of Other Cultures (Ted Ward, Holt)
A compilation of games which are played in non-American cultures.

Peace Child (Don Richardson, Regal)
An exciting story of God's message of salvation and how it was explained through the use of cultural traditions.

BEHIND THE BARRIERS

SERVING THE POOR　　　　　　　　　　　　　　　　　　　　MATTHEW 25:31-46

SESSION 11

AND YOU VISITED ME!

CAN I REALLY SERVE JESUS IN PERSON?

KEY CONCEPT	Jesus Christ is served as we reach out to those in need.
GOAL	This session is designed to motivate your young people spiritually to care for the needy.
OVERVIEW	If we think of serving the poor, the homeless, the imprisoned, or the naked just for the sake of being benevolent, our motivation will grow weak and eventually cease. In this session, students learn that seeing the poor and needy the way that Jesus sees them is the only way to keep on reaching out and serving. We must be aware of the need to do outreach as an expression of our love for Jesus to the point that we serve others as we would serve Him.
TIME REQUIRED	40-55 minutes
MATERIALS CHECKLIST	Materials needed for basic session: ___ Handout (*Test Yourself*) ___ Bibles and pens ___ Response cards (*Action Item*) Materials needed for optional activities: ___ Handout (*Finish These Sentences*)
JUNIOR HIGH ADAPTATION	The only adaptation you will need to make for use with junior highers is related to the applications. Make sure you have some concrete suggestions that you can make at the close of this session. Opportunities to serve the poor or visit prisoners are harder to come by for junior highers, so you and your coleaders must work to come up with suggestions that your junior highers can actively pursue.

SESSION OUTLINE | TIPS FOR LEADERS

WARM-UP

Optional Openers

Agree/Disagree (5 minutes)

Say: **Nobel prize winner Mother Teresa works among the poorest of the poor people in India. One of the operations of the Sisters of Mercy is a house for the terminally ill and dying. When asked why she does this, Mother Teresa simply responds: "Because I see Christ in these people, and I want to comfort them as I would comfort Him."**

Do you agree with her viewpoint? Why or why not?

Keep the discussion focused on Mother Teresa's statement. Don't get sidetracked into a discussion of your differences with her theology.

Finish These Sentences (5 minutes)

Say: **Today we are going to take a look at the way that Jesus views the poorest people, but first we should find out what we think.**

To get your own ideas flowing, think (or write) how you would finish these sentences:

1. When I think of prisoners, I immediately think of . . .
2. If I saw a naked person on my street, I would . . .
3. A smelly street person causes me to . . .
4. Being around retarded people makes me feel . . .
5. If a beggar came to my front door, I would . . .
6. A poorly dressed vagrant, sitting in the front row of our church service, would cause our church to . . .
7. If I went out to my car one morning and found a vagabond sleeping in the backseat, I would . . .
8. When someone approaches me on the street to beg from me, my first reaction is to . . .
9. If a kid at school (whom I hardly knew) asked me if he could stay over at my house because he had no home, I would . . .
10. Seeing a bag lady immediately makes me . . .

Having these sentences printed on a handout will help get everyone to respond, rather than a few (which will happen if you do the responses orally).

Close this exercise by saying: **Most of us are similar in our responses. We laugh or criticize; we would call the cops or at least ignore the poorest people around us. The Bible, however, says that our viewpoint needs changing, and the Bible study we will do later will help us.**

Test Yourself (10 minutes)

Say: **Before we embark on a Bible study on the person who is already needy, let's do some self-evaluation to see how we are doing so far.**

Score your own commitment to serving the poor by answering yes or no to these statements (you get 10 points for every positive answer); be honest.
____ I visit lonely people on a regular basis.
____ When I see a poor person, I immediately think, "That could be Jesus; how can I help him?"
____ If I see a poorly dressed person, I ask him/her if I can give some of my extra clothes.
____ I am consistent in listening to people who want to talk about their problems.
____ Writing encouragement letters to prisoners is one of my regular habits.
____ I try to do something to serve the poor at least once a month.

If you do *Finish These Sentences* on a handout, then put this test on the other side of the sheet to reduce your use of paper.

| TIPS FOR LEADERS | SESSION OUTLINE |

___ When I get some extra money, I immediately think, "How can I use this to help others?"
___ Each time I see a lonely person wandering the streets, I ask him/her home for dinner.
___ I pray every day for the homeless and poor of _____ (use the name of a nearby city).
___ I love to visit my grandparents because I know that they are lonely for my attention.

Scores: 80-100—You are a "Good Samaritan," and you probably do not need this session.
  40-70 —You are an "OK Samaritan," and this seminar is needed to give you some fresh ideas.
  0-30 —You have a ways to go in terms of caring, and this session will definitely help you get started.

WORKOUT

The Big Question (3-5 minutes)

Say: **There are thousands of poor and homeless people in our country and in our world. Millions go without food, and tens of millions are not adequately dressed. We cannot change everything all at once, but we can change some things. But before we think about changing anything, we need to know why we do what we do. So, here is the big question: What is our number one reason for seeking to help or serve the poor and destitute?** (Record answers on a chalkboard or overhead.)

You may get various answers here, ranging from "To serve Jesus" to "Because we have so much." Listen to all of the answers, but close by saying: **There are many good reasons to help the hurting or serve the poor, but the Bible cites the most powerful reason: we serve these people because by serving them we are (in a mysterious way) serving Jesus Himself. Let's read about this.**

Have a student read if possible.

Read (in the whole group) Matthew 25:31-46.

Group Study (20 minutes)

One leader per group is ideal.

Divide students into groups of at least five per group. Assign them the task of rereading the passage and then fulfilling one of these assignments:

If groups are small, tell students they must play multiple parts. You can help them by giving them construction paper on which to write titles of the different needy people named in the passage to use as labels.

Assignment 1: Act out the passage.
Assignment 2: Write an obituary which announces the earthly death of one whom Jesus would label a "sheep."
Assignment 3: Write an obituary which announces the earthly death of one whom Jesus would call a "goat."
Assignment 4: Make a list of all the actions that Jesus mentions and try to give a modern-day equivalent of what you (or your group) could do to serve Jesus.
Assignment 5: Write a complaint letter from one of the "goats" which defends the reasons why he thinks he should get to go to heaven, and then write Jesus' response.

SESSION OUTLINE

WRAP-UP

Talk-to (5 minutes)

Say: **The comments of Jesus in this chapter are very strong, and taken by themselves, they may cause us to start wondering, "Am I a Christian? I've never visited a prisoner." On the other hand, we may gain a false confidence and say, "I help poor people all the time; I must be on my way to heaven for sure."**

The passage in Matthew 25 is not to be taken by itself. We must keep it in the overall context of Scripture. In the context of the whole Bible, Matthew 25 is not a teaching of Jesus on the basis of salvation. Instead, it is a teaching of Jesus on how those who are saved really act. From it, we must remember two big lessons:
1. **The primary *motivation* for service to others must be to serve Jesus. If we serve Him, we can know that He takes notice and will reward such behavior in heaven. If we serve others just to gain their appreciation, we will get discouraged and quit because they will not respond as we want them to.**
2. **Jesus is saying that the *lifestyle* of a true believer in Him is characterized by concern for the "down-and-out" person—the hungry, lonely, ill-clothed, or destitute. As His followers, we must make choices to care for those in great need.**

Action Item (2 minutes)

Instruct students to fill in this statement and apply it this week:
Based on what Matthew 25 teaches, this week I am going to serve Jesus in this way:

TIPS FOR LEADERS

A 3x5 card that students can carry with them for the week in their pockets or wallets is ideal.

Options for Further Study

Option 1—Following up this session with some practical action often helps students increase their concern for the poor and needy. Some good follow-up ideas include:
- A visit to a nursing home or hospital (ask nurses to identify the patients who never get visits and visit them)
- Collecting eyeglasses and sending them to various missions (see *Ideas for Social Action* by Tony Campolo, p. 50)
- Doing a food collection for the poor
- Serving as waiters or waitresses at a city soup kitchen

Option 2—A study of some of the prophets with respect to the issues of the rich, the poor, and justice is enlightening and convicting. See books like *Rich Christians in an Age of Hunger* (Ronald Sider, InterVarsity Press) for ideas.

Additional Resources

Evangelicals for Social Actions (P.O. Box 12336, Philadelphia, PA 19144)
Has some good resources available for those desiring to serve the poor.

Cry Justice! The Bible on Hunger and Poverty (Ronald Sider, Paulist)
A compilation of Scripture verses according to topics related to the poor and the oppressed.

BEHIND THE BARRIERS

ACROSS SOCIAL BARRIERS   SELECTED PASSAGES

SESSION 12

LEPERS—IN MY WORLD?

HOW CAN I HELP THE REALLY HURTING PERSON?

KEY CONCEPT

We should reach out to rather than avoid the person in desperate need.

GOAL

This session shows that people in the greatest need are often the most responsive to outreach.

OVERVIEW

The retarded, the destitute, and the crippled are often scary to us. We do not know how to respond to their handicaps, so we shy away and leave them isolated. This session focuses on the real needs and feelings of the hurting person and shows young people how to start the process of outreach.

TIME REQUIRED

40-65 minutes

MATERIALS CHECKLIST

Materials needed for basic session:
____ Bibles
____ Pens
____ Quiz *(Multiple Choice Bible Test)*

JUNIOR HIGH ADAPTATION

The optional *Imagine* exercise is useful, though the *Opinion Poll* might be too advanced for use with junior highers. This session has a lot of discussion and study-oriented exercises, so you may want to interject some activities that allow for physical movement so that your junior highers are still attentive at the close of this session. This session also has a few vocabulary words (destitute, contracted, etc.) that might need revision.

SESSION OUTLINE | TIPS FOR LEADERS

WARM-UP

Optional Openers

Imagine (10 minutes)

Say: **Most of us spend our time thinking about ourselves, but there are many people less fortunate than we are. We need to understand how they feel so we can care for them as we would like to be cared for if we were in their positions.**

Instruct students that they are to imagine themselves in various circumstances and then consider the top three problems they would confront each day and the primary way they would like others to care. You should set up a response chart as follows:

| Imagine you are . . . | Your top three concerns would be: | You would like someone to care for you by: |

1. Confined to a wheelchair
2. Blind
3. Desperately poor
4. Living on the streets
5. Deaf
6. Hungry (have not eaten in 4 days)
7. Lonely (no friends)
8. Unemployed

Your group's responses can be recorded on a chalkboard or on an overhead transparency.

You may want to add categories to the "Imagine you are . . ." column to identify needs in the area where you live.

Opinion Poll (10 minutes)

Find out the opinions of your group toward the really hurting person by asking them to give their opinions in response to the following "Why?" questions:

1. Why do we hate it when someone begs us for money?
2. Why do we feel weird if we walk by a drunken man in the gutter?
3. Why are we so aware of people's clothing, especially if they are dressed poorly?
4. Why would your family feel awkward if a poor man knocked at your door and asked if he could stay the night?
5. Why do people ignore others who are crying out for help?
6. Why do we stare at people with physical handicaps?
7. Why do poor people stay poor rather than just going out to get a job?
8. Why don't rich people simply give their extra money to the poor to relieve their suffering?
9. Why do people sometimes cross the street when they see a blind person coming toward them (with either a walking stick or a seeing-eye dog)?
10. Why does it sometimes irritate us when someone calls us up for help in an emergency?

As you do this exercise, do not let answers get long and evolve into a debate. Have students share their answers and encourage them to differ without arguing. Keep the discussion moving.

Father Damien Case Study (10-15 minutes)

Start by saying: **There once was a missionary by the name of Father Damien who was told by his church to go to Hawaii. That's the good news. The bad news is that he went as a missionary to a leper colony on the island of Molokai. When he went there, over 800 patients were together without**

57

supervision and without hope. Over 200 patients per year were dying. Father Damien's work went on for 10 years before it became most effective. In 1885, 12 years after starting his work at the leper colony, Father Damien was diagnosed as having contracted leprosy himself. It was after this diagnosis that Father Damien's work received the greatest recognition and experienced the greatest success.

Discussion Questions

1. Why do you think Father Damien's success increased after he contracted leprosy?
2. Does his example mean that we must become just like the people we are trying to reach (poor, destitute, lepers, blind, etc.)?
3. What are some ways that we can identify with poor people or hurting people so that they know we care?
4. Do you think Father Damien did the right thing? (Would *you* have gone if you knew that you would contract leprosy?)

WORKOUT

Multiple Choice Bible Test (20 minutes)

The quiz below should be prepared as a handout and passed out to individuals (or groups). Answers are (in consecutive order): c, a, d, a, b, c, d, a, d, b, b, c, a, b, d, d, b, c, d, b.

Multiple Choice Bible Test

Read the following passages and try to answer the multiple choice questions that follow.

Read Luke 19:1-10.
1. Zaccheus was a
    a. garbage collector.
    b. coin collector.
    c. tax collector.
    d. dust collector.
2. Zaccheus was also
    a. short.
    b. tall.
    c. fat.
    d. thin.
3. Zaccheus had become rich by
    a. operating a tree-climbing company.
    b. honest, hard work.
    c. investing in real estate.
    d. cheating others.
4. As a tax collector and employee of Rome, Zaccheus would have been
    a. hated by his countrymen.
    b. unknown by his countrymen.
    c. on the cover of *People* magazine (Jewish edition).
    d. a welcome guest at any party.
5. Jesus reached out to Zaccheus because he was
    a. rich.
    b. lost.
    c. short.
    d. known for hosting good lunches.

If you work in groups, try to encourage students to read the passages rather than just listening passively to another student reading.

Some of the answers are intentionally humorous to keep students interested.

SESSION OUTLINE | **TIPS FOR LEADERS**

Read Mark 10:46-52.
6. Bartimaeus was a
   a. roadside vegetable salesman.
   b. crippled man.
   c. roadside beggar.
   d. deaf-mute.
7. He heard about Jesus and called out for
   a. attention.
   b. pizza.
   c. healing.
   d. mercy.
8. He kept on crying out in spite of the fact that
   a. people tried to silence him.
   b. he had a terrible sore throat.
   c. Jesus was two miles away.
   d. he was done working for the day.
9. We can assume that Bartimaeus was pretty unpopular because
   a. he was blind.
   b. he was a beggar.
   c. people were telling him to shut up.
   d. all of the above.
10. Jesus reached out to Bart so that he
    a. would stop begging.
    b. could gain his sight.
    c. would stop crying out.
    d. would follow Him.

Read James 2:1-9.
11. The basic problem James addresses is
    a. equal rights.
    b. favoritism in favor of the rich.
    c. rich/poor relationships.
    d. the way to dress for church services.
12. James writes that discrimination against the poor is to become
    a. just like a rich man.
    b. an enemy of God.
    c. judges of others, with bad motives ourselves.
    d. a fashion expert.
13. Ironically, the rich people who get favored may be
    a. the people who get money out of us by unfair practices.
    b. poor people in disguise.
    c. members of organized crime.
    d. not sincere about their faith in God.
14. In contrast, the poor people we might judge are actually
    a. the minister and his family.
    b. people who are rich before God because they know their need.
    c. trend-setters in new styles of clothing.
    d. rich people in disguise.
15. Showing such favoritism is to
    a. make a big mistake.
    b. sin and overlook our "neighbors."
    c. dishonor God's specially chosen people.
    d. all of the above.

Read Luke 16:19-26.
16. The rich man was so rich that
    a. he wore purple clothes and fine linen.
    b. he spilled enough food to feed another person.
    c. he had a feast every day.
    d. all of the above.

TIPS FOR LEADERS | SESSION OUTLINE

17. Lazarus was so poor, on the other hand, that
    a. he could not even pay attention.
    b. he depended on dogs to clean his skin sores.
    c. he had no home.
    d. he was on welfare.
18. Lazarus died and went to
    a. heaven.
    b. Paradise.
    c. Abraham's side.
    d. Hawaii.
19. The rich man went to
    a. a place of torture.
    b. a very hot place.
    c. Hades.
    d. all of the above.
20. Abraham explains the situation as follows:
    a. all poor go to heaven; all rich go to hell.
    b. the rich man got all of the good things in the first life.
    c. Lazarus got saved because he was poor.
    d. none of the above.

Explain that we are all lost, but the people Jesus saves are the ones who know and admit the fact that they are lost.

After students finish the quiz, go over it together and reiterate the main point from Luke 19:10—that Jesus came to seek and to save the lost. The poor and needy are special to God because they know their need of Him.

WRAP-UP

Closing Scripture (5 minutes)

Before the concluding words, read Mark 2:15-17 and say: **Jesus came for the people who recognize their need of Him. The social, economic, and physical outcasts were all His special concerns. The social rejects like Zaccheus, the economic losers like Lazarus, and the physically damaged like Bartimaeus were all His special concern because these needy people (like the sinners and tax collectors of Mark 2) were not afraid to ask for God's help and for mercy.**

Closing Prayer (5 minutes)

Suggesting some of the follow-up activities (see Options for Further Study) can help students to focus their prayers.

Close this session with a time of prayer when you ask for students to pray aloud about hurting people that they know they should be reaching out to.

Option for Further Study

This is a good session to use as a launching pad for an ongoing ministry at a state hospital, a soup kitchen, or some other place where you can serve the people who are most socially separated from us.

Additional Resources

How to Build a Youth Outreach Ministry (Bill Stearns, Victor Books)
Helpful in planning outreach teams and covering details on service projects.

World Relief Commission (P.O. Box WRC, Wheaton, IL 60189)
This ministry can suggest ways to start caring for refugees in your area.

SECTION 4

TO THE ENDS OF THE EARTH

Assuming that you survived section 3 and the challenges there, you are now ready to take on the world. The call of Christ to "Go" is the focus, and the next four sessions lead young people to consider what it means to be a "world Christian."

According to Jay Kesler, president of Taylor University, one of the great challenges facing teenagers and those who work with them is apathy. The attitude of today's young people, however, is not the same as the apathy of the young people of the fifties. Dr. Kesler points out that earlier generations were apathetic because they really did not know what was going on in the world. Teenagers today are different. They are apathetic because they know about the immense issues of the world, but they do not think they can make a difference. It just seems too big to them.

As you start these four sessions, it is important that you maintain the "You Can Make a Difference" attitude. An average young person will hear much of the information of these sessions with skepticism (like the title of session 15—"But I Don't Care Where Burkina Faso Is"). As the group leader, you must seek creative and effective ways to challenge your group members with the realization that they can indeed make a difference in the *world* for Christ.

Student responses may vary widely with respect to these sessions. Some will be anxious to hear more and will actually be sensing God's call into missionary work during these sessions. Others may be interested but yield no immediate response. Remember that your goal should be to get young people to think in enlarged ways about their world. As you are communicating the "You Can Make a Difference" theme to them, you must remember that *you* can make a difference in the lives of the students you are leading.

TO THE ENDS OF THE EARTH

BUILDING A WORLDVIEW SELECTED PASSAGES

SESSION 13

EXPAND YOUR HORIZONS

WHAT DO I HAVE TO DO WITH THE BIG WORLD?

KEY CONCEPT — As Christians, we must think about where we fit into God's worldwide plan.

GOAL — This session challenges students to start developing a perspective of and concern for the world.

OVERVIEW — We can all fall prey to the temptation to care only about our own little worlds rather than focusing our attention (and prayers and actions) outward. By revealing not only the scope of world need but also God's concern for the world and a few practical ways to start being involved, this session starts the process of helping teenagers become "world Christians."

TIME REQUIRED — 40-55 minutes

MATERIALS CHECKLIST

Materials needed for basic session:
____ Bibles
____ Pencils
____ Crossword puzzle handout

Materials needed for optional activities:
____ 2 copies of skit *(How to Live on $100 a Year)*
____ Chalkboard (To record discussion answers)

JUNIOR HIGH ADAPTATION — The skit is probably applicable and understandable for junior highers, though they may struggle with the crossword puzzle. Also, look over this session in advance to check out any vocabulary words that students may not understand.

TIPS FOR LEADERS

SESSION OUTLINE

WARM-UP

Optional Openers

How to Live on $100 a Year (10 minutes)

Have two students prepared beforehand to perform this skit so that you get the full impact.

This skit requires no props, no costumes, and no set. It has only two characters, and can be performed in a chancel, in a family room, or in a classroom.
(Two people meet. "B" looks downcast.)

A: Hey, Friend, you look troubled. What's your problem?
B: Money.
A: Can't make ends meet, huh?
B: Meet? I can't even get them in shouting distance. The way prices are going up . . .
A: (Interrupts.) Friend, have I ever got the program for you! It's called "How to live on one hundred dollars a year."
B: One hundred dollars a year? Is that possible?
A: Sure. Half the people in the world do it all the time.
B: How do I start?
A: First, get rid of all your furniture except one table and one chair. That cuts down not only on payments, but also on cleaning supplies.
B: Cuts down on guests too, but where do I sit to watch TV?
A: No TV, no radio, no books, or magazines. You're cutting down, remember?
B: Yeah, but . . . well, I guess I go out for my entertainment?
A: If you like. But give away all your clothes except one outfit—your oldest. And keep one pair of shoes for the head of the family.
B: You mean everybody else goes barefoot? I might like that for a while, but I don't know about making it a regular practice. What else?
A: Shut off your electricity, water, and gas. Think of all the money you'll save! And disconnect the phone—don't forget that.
B: How will we run the dishwasher, toaster, hair dryer?
A: Send those to Goodwill. You can't afford them on one hundred dollars a year. And as for baths, use the rain.
B: How will we cook?
A: Gather scraps of wood and things that will burn. It's amazing how much waste wood you can find if you try. But donate most of your food to a crisis center. Keep only a small bag of flour, some sugar and salt, a few moldy potatoes, a handful of onions, and some dried beans. Meal planning becomes a breeze!
B: (Doubtfully.) Is that a balanced diet?
A: Friend, on one hundred dollars a year, you can't have everything.
B: But what if I get sick? I can't even call a doctor—no phone.
A: Use the midwife in a clinic about 10 miles away. Half the world does. And if you need a doctor, there's one farther down the road.
B: How long would it take to get to a doctor—driving, I mean?
A: Driving? Oh—I forgot. You'll need to give up your car. They eat up your income.
B: (Sarcastic.) What'll we do with the garage—rent it out?
A: No, live in it. Get rid of the house too. Of course your garage is larger than the ordinary house allowed in this program, but since you don't have a toolshed . . .
B: Hey, this isn't living, it's . . . What do I do about school? I can't walk there on an empty stomach, in my oldest clothes without a bath, and expect them to let me stay very long. I suppose this program thought of that too?
A: Sure. Your best bet is to become a tenant farmer. With three acres and a good year, you can expect from one to three hundred dollars worth of cash crops. Pay the landlord a third and the moneylender 10 percent, and you get what's left.
B: Moneylender? Oh, come on. Why do I need a moneylender?

| SESSION OUTLINE | TIPS FOR LEADERS |

A: Well, some years there'll be a drought, or maybe a flood. Then you won't get a hundred dollars. And you need a hundred dollars to live on this program effectively.
B: Yeah, I can see I do. What about saving for my old age?
A: Well, there's bad news and good news. You can't afford insurance, pension plans, or savings accounts, which is the bad news. But the good news is that you won't need them.
B: Yeah? Why not?
A: Because under this program you can count on living 25 to 30 years less.
B: Oh, that's great. Hey, look, forget it, OK? I appreciate your trying to help and all, but suddenly I don't think I need help after all. My bills look pretty small. (Starts to walk away and mutters to self.) That's not living. It's barely existing. In fact, I'm not sure people could live like that. (Exits.)
A: In our economy we can't really live on a hundred dollars a year. But could we live on a hundred dollars a year less? That's about nine dollars a month, or two dollars a week. Would that require sacrifice? Would we even miss it? Yet think what could be done for the world's hungry if each person or even each family represented in this room gave a hundred dollars a year to fight hunger. Shall we?

(Taken from *HUNGER: Understanding the Crisis through Games, Dramas & Songs,* by Patricia Houck Sprinkle, copyright John Knox Press, 1980. Used by permission.)

Discussion (5 minutes)

Say to your students: **Dr. Tony Campolo has been telling a lot of young people, "You can make a difference." Do you really believe that *you* can make a difference in our world? If no, why? If yes, how can you make a difference?**

Recording discussion answers on a chalkboard helps students share some good ideas for involvement.

Crossword Puzzle (15 minutes)

Start by saying: **For many of us, the needs of our world are so immense that we do not even want to try. We think, "It's too big, too awesome," and we give up. The Bible, on the other hand, is full of examples of people who made a difference, and it commands us to do the same. Start getting the big picture by completing this missions crossword puzzle.**

It may be best to do the crossword puzzle in the big group rather than individually so as not to alienate students who know little of the Bible.

65

| TIPS FOR LEADERS | SESSION OUTLINE |

DOWN (Old Testament)
1. He could have been a "missionary," but he failed.
2. She acted and made it necessary to have missions.
4. He was the one through whom "all the nations of the earth would be blessed."
5. She was a missionary to the Persian king.
6. God told Israel to be a "light to the _____."
10. But God told Israel to reach out to the "_____ and strangers."
11. He was a missionary in Egypt.
12. The people of Israel were hesitant to "witness" to these people.

ACROSS (New Testament)
1. All Christians are to be known by this quality.
3. The greatest missionary in the Book of Acts.
5. A Greek word which we translate the "nations."
7. He failed on his first trip as a missionary.
8. He was timid, but he became a missionary to Ephesus.
9. All Christians are commanded to _____.
12. When we go, we bring the _____.
13. This is where Paul almost made it to before he was captured.
14. Nickname of the apostle who went to India, according to legend.
15. God does not want any to _____.

After students complete the puzzle, go over the correct answers: Down—(1) Lot; (2) Eve; (4) Abraham; (5) Esther; (6) nations; (10) aliens; (11) Joseph; (12) Gentiles. Across—(1) love; (3) Paul; (5) *ethne;* (7) Mark; (8) Timothy; (9) go; (12) Gospel; (13) Spain; (14) Tom; (15) perish. (You may also want to comment on specific people—Esther, Joseph, Mark, etc.—and use them as examples.)

WORKOUT

Read and Discuss (15 minutes)

Encourage students to read the passages.

Keeping your group together (or, if your group is large, using small groups), read and respond to these verses and questions:

Genesis 12:1-4
What aspects of God's promise appeal to you? (Some may like the idea of leaving home; most will like the promises of greatness and fame.) **What effect will Abraham have on the rest of the world?** (He will be God's agent of blessing.) **If this promise is to be fulfilled today, how will God bless "all the families of the earth" through Abraham?** (We are the children of Abraham through our faith in God; *we* are supposed to be a blessing to the whole world.)

Isaiah 42:6
How does God want to use His people Israel? (As a covenant [or promise] to others and a light [an expression of His truth] to all nations.) **What promise does God give to Israel as they fulfill this role?** (He promises to hold them by the hand and watch over them. In other words, He promises security.) **In what ways can you and I be "lights" to the nations?** (Students may have no ideas, or they may talk about supporting missionaries or raising money for hungry people.)

Matthew 24:14
What prerequisite does Jesus establish for His return? (He says that all the world must hear the Gospel first.) **Why do you think Jesus will delay His coming like this?** (He desires all to hear the Good News of His love.) **How can people hear this Good News?** (From someone else who already knows it—read Romans 10:13-15.)

Revelation 7:9-10
At the close of the ages, who stands before God singing praises to Him? (Great numbers from all nations and tribes and languages.) **How do you think these people came to know Jesus so that they could sing His praises?** (Someone on earth must have told them.)

WRAP-UP

Talk-to (10 minutes)

Say: **We all have the tendency to be selfish and to think only about ourselves. (If you don't believe me, ask yourself this question: "When I see a group picture that I am in, who do I look for first?" Our selfishness can be cured, however, when we start to get God's big picture of love for the whole world. Our day-to-day concerns can be minimized as we see the incredible needs of people around us—in our own country, but especially in the poorer countries of the world.**

But, you might say, how do I begin? How can I make any difference in a world of 4 billion people, where there are over 1 billion hungry people and over 2 billion who have no one to tell them about Jesus Christ? This is the tough part—seeing where we play a part. Here are a few suggestions of action that you can start taking now:

1. *Pray.* **Start praying about the world. Ask God to show you what to do. Pray for a specific country—like North Korea or Albania or Libya—where there are few, if any, Christians.**
2. *Research.* **Find out more about needs in the world today.**
3. *Give.* **Maybe you don't have a lot of money, but you can help people by giving of what you have. A few dollars a month, pooled together with a few friends, could support a needy family or child in another part of the world.**
4. *Tell others.* **Getting excited about God's big plan for the world is contagious. If you start telling others of God's love for the world, they can get excited with you and start praying, researching, giving too.**
5. *Start small.* **You don't have to save the whole world by yourself, but you can do something. World Vision has a poster that says, "How do you help 1 million starving people? One at a time."**

God's heart and concern are for the whole world. If we are to follow Him wholeheartedly, we too must be "world Christians." As we start caring about the big world out there, realizing that God wants people to come to know Him, He will use us to change the world!

Option for Further Study

Invite someone who has served in missions overseas to share how one or two people have made a difference in another part of the world.

Additional Resources

World Christian Magazine (P.O. Box 5199, Chatsworth, CA 91313)
Designed to challenge young people to grow to be "world Christians."

In the Gap (David Bryant, InterVarsity Press)
A helpful tool for building missions vision, especially among leaders.

Newsletters like *The Church Around the World* (Tyndale), *In Other Words* (Wycliffe Bible Translators), or *World Vision* magazine can supply you with valuable examples of people making a difference around the world.

TIPS FOR LEADERS

This is a good opportunity to share an anecdote about the work of some Bible translator or other missionary who brought God's Word for the first time to a tribe.

Encourage students to take notes on these five suggestions.

TO THE ENDS OF THE EARTH

PERSONALIZING MISSIONS   SELECTED PASSAGES

SESSION 14

MISSIONS—A DAILY AFFAIR

HOW DOES WORLD MISSIONS APPLY TO MY LIFE?

KEY CONCEPT | To be world-minded Christians, we must incorporate world concerns into our lives every day.

GOAL | This session suggests a variety of ways that students can start making world missions relevant to daily living.

OVERVIEW | Our prayers, thoughts, and personal learning often forget the fact that there is a big world to be involved in. This session shows how the enormous realities of world needs and world events can be integrated into the normal affairs of our daily lives, our prayers, and our thinking. By gaining a view of the world, young people are challenged to keep their own lives, needs, and problems in proper perspective.

TIME REQUIRED | 50-70 minutes

MATERIALS CHECKLIST | Materials needed for basic session:
____ Newspapers from the past week
____ Scissors
____ Bibles
____ Pens and paper

Materials needed for optional activities:
____ Quiz (*Knowledge Check-up*)
____ Prayer cards or information about an "adopted" missionary
____ Excerpts from the biographies of George Mueller or Hudson Taylor

JUNIOR HIGH ADAPTATION | Making this session effective with junior highers depends on the involvement of adult leaders. If there are adults to guide the activities and prayertime, then the program should go well. If there are not enough adults, then you should consider modifying the session a little, perhaps by encouraging students to write out a prayer for a missionary and sending it (as opposed to the more general prayertime suggested in this session).

SESSION OUTLINE | TIPS FOR LEADERS

WARM-UP

Optional Openers

Knowledge Check-up (5-10 minutes)

Say: **The Bible is full of examples of the ways we are supposed to act as Christians in response to the needs of the world around us. How much do you know about practical "world Christian" living?** (Answers are in parentheses.)

(b) 1. Our first priority as Christians is to
   a. go to be missionaries.
   b. give ourselves to the Lord.
   c. make sure our own needs are met.
                (See 2 Corinthians 8:5)

(c) 2. God promises a day when
   a. everybody will be Christians.
   b. all the poor will overtake the rich.
   c. the earth will be filled with the knowledge of Him.
                (See Habakkuk 2:14)

(a) 3. One example of God using a little gift to do a great work is
   a. the story of the boy's loaves and fishes.
   b. the story of the mustard seed.
   c. the story of the Good Samaritan.
                (See John 6:5-14)

(b) 4. God prefers
   a. religious services.
   b. shared bread.
   c. frequent fasting.
                (See Isaiah 58:5-7)

(b) 5. After we commit to help someone we should
   a. give no matter what.
   b. give generously as we would to Jesus.
   c. give when things are going well for us.
                (See 2 Corinthians 9:7)

After the quiz, you may want to reiterate that God desires us to be involved with the needs and opportunities around the world.

Testimony (10 minutes)

If possible, have a missionary on furlough share a testimony of how God directed him or her to the particular mission field on which he or she now serves. Ask the missionary to share in particular about the ways that brought him or her from the United States into missions.

Newspaper Search (15 minutes)

Hand out a copy of a daily newspaper from the past week to each student, and give each a pair of scissors. Then ask students to go through the paper and cut out every article they can find related to international affairs.

Having this quiz on the top half of a handout makes the quiz easier to administer and gives students some space to take notes later in the session.

If you do have a visiting missionary speak, make sure to brief him or her on your group and offer some tips regarding talking to teenagers. Don't assume that the missionary is accustomed to addressing young people.

Give out recent copies of the newspaper, and eliminate sections like the sports, movie ads, or funnies so as to keep your students from getting off the track.

TIPS FOR LEADERS	SESSION OUTLINE

After about eight minutes of cutting, ask students to get together to share what they have found with three or four others. Chances are, one or two international events will dominate the news stories. Ask students to concentrate on the one or two countries that have been most in the news that week.

When students have decided the countries on which they would focus, ask them to list what they think would be the primary prayer concerns for missionaries and national Christians in that country. After completing this task, have students share their answers.

Instruct students to hold on to these ideas so that they can compare notes later (after the Workout).

WORKOUT

Start by saying: **We often wonder where we fit into God's worldwide concern, especially in day-to-day experience. One of the ways that we can make missions a part of our day-to-day growth as Christians is prayer.**

Discussion Groups (15 minutes)

One leader per group is desirable.

Divide students into groups of three or four. Then assign each group three verses related to prayer. Each group is then to look up the verses and answer these questions:
1. What promise or command does God give us about prayer?
2. How should these verses change our thinking about prayer?
3. In what ways should these verses apply to our prayers for the world or for missionaries?

Make sure to prepare your leaders in advance of this session so that they are familiar with the texts being studied.

Some sample verses you can choose from are:

Philippians 4:19	Philippians 4:6-7
Ephesians 3:20-21	James 5:13-16
Jeremiah 33:3	Colossians 4:2-4
Mark 9:23	Matthew 9:36-38
Isaiah 65:24	Ephesians 6:18-20
John 16:24	1 Timothy 2:1-4

After each group has answered the questions, have them share their answers for the benefit of the whole group. (Writing their answers on the chalkboard or on an overhead transparency can help the whole group see the answers and take notes.)

WRAP-UP

Prayertime (10 minutes)

Instruct students that it is OK to open their eyes periodically as they pray so that they can pray according to the promises they just studied, which are now listed on the chalkboard or overhead.

Say to your group: **Do you remember the countries or areas of the world (*Newspaper Search*) that have been especially turbulent this week? Now that you know some of God's commands and promises related to prayer, spend some time in your groups praying specifically for Christians and Christian missionaries in these countries.**

Talk-to (10 minutes)

Your enthusiasm is very important for an effective summary.

Say: **On a daily basis, the primary way that we can be involved around the world is through our prayers, and yet very few of us take advantage of this privilege.**

Imagine for a moment that the President of the United States called you on the phone and asked you to fly to Washington, D.C. to consult with him

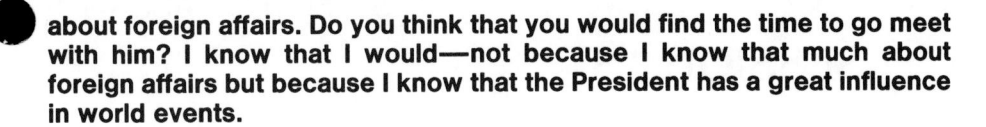

about foreign affairs. Do you think that you would find the time to go meet with him? I know that I would—not because I know that much about foreign affairs but because I know that the President has a great influence in world events.

This is the privilege that we have every day as Christians. God—the all-powerful ruler of the universe—invites us to pray, to consult with Him—about world events. We need to take Him up on this invitation for at least two reasons.

First, like the boy who offered his loaves and fishes, we can see God do a mighty work through our little offering—our prayers. Through our prayers, God will act and, as a result, we play a part in influencing world history.

Second, on a more personal level, praying about the needs of the world will change us. As we start praying for world situations—like hunger or earthquakes or hopelessness or wars—we begin to get a better perspective on our own lives. Maybe our problems are just not that big after all. As we learn to trust God with the big issues of our world, we can also trust Him with our personal needs and concerns.

Close in prayer.

Options for Further Study

Option 1—Sharing selections out of one of the many biographies of either Hudson Taylor or George Mueller can be excellent for stimulating excitement about the ways that God answers prayers.

Option 2—This is perhaps the best session to introduce a "Missions Adoption" program in which your youth group "adopts" a foreign missionary. Prayer cards, letters, and reports from this missionary can inspire your young people to pray and—through the adopted missionary—to have an impact on some other part of the world. (Good "adoption" programs usually begin with prayer but soon evolve into correspondence, missionary visits, and even gifts from the youth group to the missionary you have adopted.)

Additional Resources

Bread for the World (207 East 16th St., New York, NY 10003)
A good resource for teaching others practical ways that students can work to change the plight of the hungry.

World Vision (Box O, Monrovia, CA 91101)
A hunger and relief organization with lots of practical ideas for involving young people in missions projects.

What Do You Say to a Hungry World? (Stan Mooneyham, Word)
A study of world hunger designed to make the facts and figures personal and to encourage people to respond to the needs they hear about.

Frontier Fellowship (U.S. Center for World Mission, 1605 E. Elizabeth, Pasadena, CA 91101)
This monthly prayer guide has a devotional every day as well as some instructions for prayer for "hidden peoples," those that have never heard of Jesus Christ.

A personal example of how a worldview helped you get perspective on a personal problem is very effective at this point.

TO THE ENDS OF THE EARTH

BUILDING COMPASSION SELECTED PASSAGES

SESSION 15

BUT I DON'T CARE WHERE BURKINA FASO IS

MISSIONS IS SO VAST—HOW CAN I CARE ABOUT IT ALL?

KEY CONCEPT

God doesn't expect us to be responsible for the whole world.

GOAL

Students will learn that caring for the world means involvement, but not 100 percent perfect knowledge.

OVERVIEW

The world's needs are so great that we can never care for every need nor every person. This vastness, however, is no excuse for failing to care and giving up on our compassion for those who are hurting or without Christ. This session focuses on the need to balance heart-felt compassion with practical involvement so that we do not get apathetic about it or overwhelmed by it all.

TIME REQUIRED

45-60 minutes

MATERIALS CHECKLIST

Materials needed for basic session:
_____ Bibles and pens
_____ Handout (*A Study in Responses*)
_____ World map (*Everything About Somewhere*)

Materials needed for optional activities:
_____ Copies of quiz (*Just Imagine It*)
_____ Copies of skit (*I Don't Care*)

JUNIOR HIGH ADAPTATION

This session may be more difficult with junior highers because they may not "feel" overwhelmed by world need. They may not know or care about needs beyond themselves. The quiz (*Just Imagine It*) and the optional skit from session 13 (*How to Live on $100 a Year*) can help to reinforce this sense of the need of others.

Junior highers may need a little help in determining a "somewhere" for which to be concerned, so it may be wise to have whole groups, along with their leaders, choose an area for which to be concerned.

SESSION OUTLINE | TIPS FOR LEADERS

WARM-UP

Optional Openers

Just Imagine It (5 minutes)

Start by saying: **Imagine what you and I would have to do to move from our country to any one of the world's poorest countries ... countries like Lesotho, Paraguay, Chad, Afghanistan, Bangladesh. Can you imagine it? Here are some questions about how you would live. How accurately can you picture it?** (Answers are in parentheses.)

(c) 1. Your home would be approximately as large as an American
    a. house.
    b. garage.
    c. toolshed.
    d. doghouse.

(b) 2. Which of the following furniture would you probably have?
    a. a table, chairs, bed, one chest
    b. a table, one chair, a few blankets
    c. a table, no chairs, a bed, and no chest
    d. a table, chairs, stove, bed, and chest

(a) 3. Your family wardrobe could consist of
    a. one outfit per person, and shoes for the head of the family.
    b. two outfits per person, including shoes.
    c. one outfit per person, and no shoes.
    d. a few worn garments.

(b) 4. In your pantry you'd probably have
    a. dried meat and a few vegetables.
    b. a little flour, salt and sugar, moldy potatoes, dried beans, and onions.
    c. only rice.
    d. dried meat, vegetables, and powdered milk.

(b) 5. You would get water from
    a. a faucet in your yard.
    b. the village well.
    c. a river.

(d) 6. You would probably own
    a. electric lights.
    b. a pet dog.
    c. a saw.
    d. no tools or pets.

(d) 7. You would get information from
    a. magazines.
    b. your radio.
    c. your TV.
    d. the village radio.

(b) 8. When you got sick, you would go to
    a. the doctor down the street.
    b. a clinic 10 miles away, run by a midwife.
    c. the hospital in the next town.
    d. heaven.

(a) 9. Your annual income would average
    a. $100-$300.
    b. $500-$1,000.
    c. $1,000-$3,000.
    d. $3,000-$5,000.

(c) 10. Your life expectancy would probably be
    a. about the same as now.
    b. 5-10 years less.
    c. 25-30 years less.
    d. 5-10 years more.

(Taken from *HUNGER: Understanding the Crisis through Games, Dramas & Songs*, by Patricia Houck Sprinkle, copyright John Knox Press, 1980. Used by permission.)

Explain to students that the purpose of this exercise is to help us understand how many people in the world really live.

TIPS FOR LEADERS | SESSION OUTLINE

Close the quiz by saying: **The answers show us that we have a very tough time identifying with the poorest people in our world. Nevertheless, we must make a choice to care for them. The Bible calls this choice compassion.**

I Don't Care (10 minutes)

This can be done as a skit with yourself and one other person. You (A) are to serve as the person full of facts; the other person (B) is responding.

- A: I see that there was another earthquake in South America today.
- B: Uh-huh (a halfhearted grunt that says, "So what!").
- A: And did you know that a tidal wave is expected in Indonesia?
- B: No (perturbed), I guess I didn't know that.
- A: It's also a fact that dozens of people will die of hunger in just the time we have this conversation.
- B: So what do you want me to do?
- A: Just listen: there are over 2 billion people who are without any knowledge of Christ and are going to hell without Him.
- B: Why are you telling me this?
- A: To make you care.
- B: Care? How can I care? It's beyond my reach, and I have enough problems of my own.
- A: But don't you realize that today in Burkina Faso . . .
- B: (Interrupts) But I don't *care* about Burkina Faso. (Walks out angrily.)

After the person exits, ask students to discuss their own feelings of frustration related to missions. You may find out that a lot of them have adopted an "I don't care" attitude simply because the world's need seems too vast.

Debate (10 minutes)

The real issue of concern for the world hinges on our attitude toward those who have never heard the Gospel. Emotions may rise when you start this debate, but it is crucial to establishing the foundations for outreach.

Make the following statement and ask students if they agree or disagree; then ask them to defend their views. Use the Bible.

Statement: People who have never heard about Jesus are condemned to eternity without Him.

WORKOUT

Definition (1 minute)

Say: **Compassion—the Greek word which we translate "compassion" (see Matthew 9:36-38 for an example)—is actually related to the word for intestines. In graphic terms, the word means that the one who is "moved with compassion" is actually so affected by what he sees or knows that his "guts" hurt or he becomes nauseated.**

A Study in Responses (15 minutes)

Say: **The Bible gives us a number of examples of specific incidents in which people were confronted with a need or opportunity and they responded. In**

Tips for Leaders (left column):

Make sure you rehearse this skit so as to show the frustration in person B.

Identifying the lack of concern in the youth group (yawns during the skit, the "Why-do-we-have-to-do-this?" attitude, etc.) can show that we all have the same problem of disinterest.

Make sure *you* know what you believe and why before you start this debate.

After the debate, make the statement: If Jesus is "the way" to God (John 14:6) and "no one comes to the Father" except through Jesus, then we do not have much hope for those without Christ. This *is* the primary motivation for all missions work.

Having a definition written on a chalkboard or on an overhead transparency will help reinforce the meaning.

One leader per group is desirable to facilitate discussion rather than a simple "fill-in-the-blank" approach to this study.

small groups complete the chart (below) with your answers (potential answers are in parentheses).

Scripture verses	People involved	Response	Motivation for the response?
1. Luke 9:49-50	(Jesus, disciples, man preaching in Jesus' name)	(Disciples wanted to forbid him)	(Jealousy?)
2. Luke 9:51-56	(Jesus, disciples, Samaritans)	(Disciples wanted to call down fire on them)	(Anger, hatred, revenge)
3. Romans 5:8	(God, Jesus, us)	(In spite of our sins, God sent Jesus)	(Love)
4. Acts 16:9-10	(Paul, Macedonians)	(He responded to the dream/call for help)	(Love, desire to obey God)
5. Luke 14:16-20	(Man throwing a party and invitees)	(They were too busy to come)	(Too busy)
6. Matthew 9:36-39	(Jesus, troubled people)	(Prayer)	(Compassion)

After the chart is completed, ask students in the small groups: **As we look at the great needs around the world, how will we respond? Will we be like any of these examples? Which of the motivations and responses do you think God wants us to have?** (3, 4, and 6) Allow time for feedback to these questions.

WRAP-UP

Talk-to (10 minutes)

Say: **We all know the frustration of hearing about needs and opportunities around the world and feeling powerless to respond. If we continue to develop this sense of helplessness, we can become apathetic.**

The word apathy comes from Greek words (a = negative; pathos = feeling) that literally mean "without feeling." We can become apathetic when we stop hurting for the poor, we stop caring about starving millions, or we just cannot take any more. Apathy makes us want to give up. Or, like the disciples, we may get so frustrated that we want God to call down fire from heaven.

The opposite of apathy for the Christian is compassion—genuine, deep concern. But we cannot have compassion about every place. We cannot reduce our lives to live like the poorest or hungriest people of the world. If we get upset stomachs about every need we see in the news, we will never again feel healthy. There are solutions, though—practical ways to maintain compassion and to keep from apathy.

First, **we can start caring about the people right around us. We may not be able to tell a tribal person in Indonesia about Jesus, but we can tell our friends (and they may not know about Jesus' love either!).**

Second, **we can pray, because this puts us in touch with the One in charge, God. We cannot care for the whole world, but we can stay in touch with the God who does. Through this contact, we can find out where we fit into His worldwide plan.**

TIPS FOR LEADERS | SESSION OUTLINE

Finally, we can get started learning about the world. One way to do this is to develop the habit of knowing "everything about somewhere, something about everywhere."

Everything About Somewhere (10 minutes)

A world map or a globe is a must for this exercise.

Explain this exercise as a way to start maintaining a practical handle on world concerns. The idea is that students will commit themselves to learning "something about everywhere" (like where Burkina Faso is) and "everything about somewhere." The focus in this closing portion of this session is the latter.

Your personal enthusiasm and example are the most important ingredients for making this work.

Encourage your students to pick a place or country in the world. This becomes their "somewhere." Then explain that this area of interest can become a topic of prayer, reading, and research. Their "somewhere" becomes a special area or people or country for which they can have compassion by really getting interested and involved. Before asking students to pick their "somewhere," share a particular place or people for whom you are praying. Tell students how you are learning about the place *(National Geographic,* the newspaper, etc.) and what you hope to do in terms of prayer for missions and compassion for that specific concern.

After students have picked a "somewhere," close with a time of prayer for these places or people.

Options for Further Study

Option 1—A book review of J. Robertson McQuilken's *The Great Omission* (Baker) can cover the five basic reasons why we have failed to fulfill Christ's Great Commission. One of the reasons he cites relates directly to this session; he says that we have not reached the world with the love of Christ because we just do not care that much. The chapter is short, yet it can stimulate greater discussion on the subject of caring.

Option 2—Do a study of the article "The Fate of Those Who've Never Heard? It Depends" (by Malcolm McVeigh, *Evangelical Missions Quarterly* [October 1985], pp. 370-379); the article discusses the various views held by evangelicals on the plight of the heathen.

Additional Resources

Peace Child (Gospel Films)
A very interesting and motivational film for young people regarding missions and the power of God to transform lives.

Obey the Vision through Prayer (InterVarsity Press)
A helpful booklet with ideas and resources designed to encourage prayer for the world.

Opengage, A Youth Guide to World Mission (John Herbert, Lutheran Church of America)
A manual for youth which is designed to stimulate awareness of and commitment to missions.

Operation World: A Handbook for World Intercession (Patrick J. Johnstone, William Carey Library)
An excellent country-by-country compilation of information about the Christian church around the world. Very helpful in the "Everything About Somewhere" exercise.

TO THE ENDS OF THE EARTH

PERSONAL RESPONSE   JONAH

SESSION 16

MY ROLE IN THE WORLD
WHERE DOES GOD WANT ME TO GO?

KEY CONCEPT — Submitting to Christ as Lord means going wherever He directs us.

GOAL — Students will be encouraged to see that God could use them at other places in the world.

OVERVIEW — Submitting to the lordship of Christ means being willing to say, "Here I am; send me," but it is not just willingness that God uses. He also works through things like ability, desire, and life situations. This session will focus on both the need to be willing to follow Jesus wherever He leads, and to understand the ways that God leads people overseas.

TIME REQUIRED — 40-70 minutes

MATERIALS CHECKLIST

Materials needed for basic session:
___ World globe (*Missions Roulette*)
___ Bibles and pens
___ Handout (*C-A-L-L*)

Materials needed for optional activities:
___ Handout (*Constellation Game*)

JUNIOR HIGH ADAPTATION — Though junior highers are a long way from making career decisions, they do need instruction on the lordship of Christ. As a result, the *Constellation Game* may not be applicable for use with them. Do not minimize this session, however, thinking, *My junior highers are not thinking about missionary service.* Many of those on the mission field today testify that they heard their first call to missionary service in their pre- or early teens.

TIPS FOR LEADERS	SESSION OUTLINE
	# WARM-UP

Optional Openers

Constellation Game (10 minutes)

God's guidance usually does not come through one avenue but through a variety of means through which He speaks. These various means, working together, form a picture in the same way various stars form the pictures we call constellations.

As you connect the dots to spell out the word "Y-O-U," you can explain that sometimes we do not see the big picture of a constellation until someone else shows us. (Example: Orion.)	Have your students brainstorm all the different ways they think God speaks, and have them put each different way beside the x's on the handout (see sample below). After they come up with enough ideas for each x, you connect the x's to spell out God's primary concern as He guides. (His primary concern is Y-O-U.)
Offering some examples of how God guides people can help the group get started.	

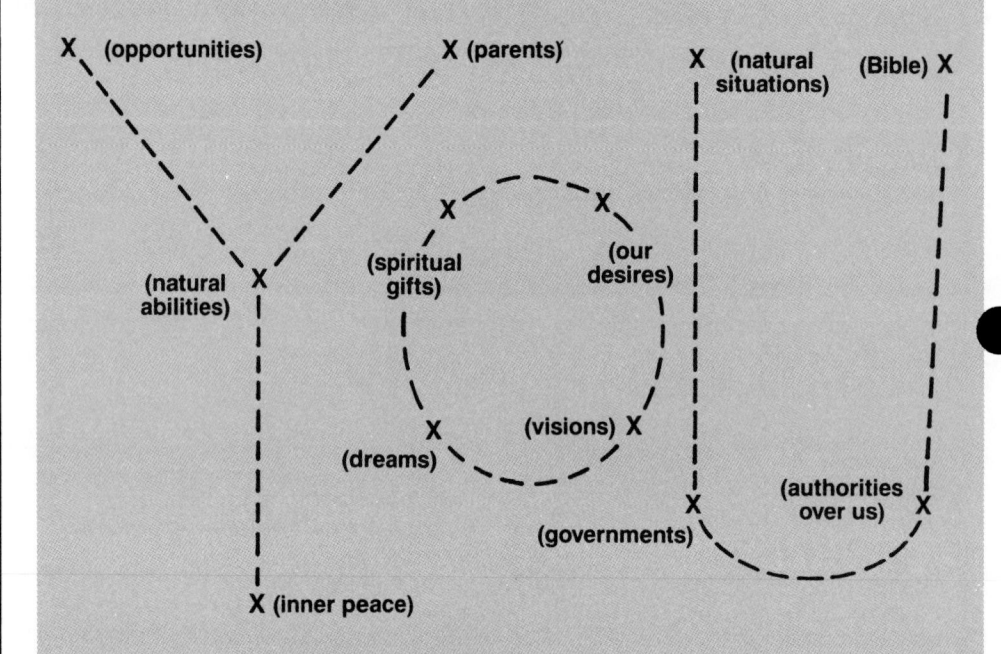

X (opportunities) X (parents) X (natural situations) (Bible) X

X (natural abilities) X (spiritual gifts) X (our desires)

X (dreams) X (visions)

X (governments) (authorities over us) X

X (inner peace)

What Would You Do? (5 minutes)

This game seeks to help students understand how they might respond to some of the "calls" God gave in the Bible.

If you have time, read or summarize the response of the person in the Scriptures listed.	Ask students: **What would you do . . .** • if God came to you via an angel and told you that you (or guys, your girlfriend) were going to have an illegitimate child that He had fathered? (See Matthew 1:18-25; Luke 1:26-38.) • if you were doing your normal work and Jesus came to you and said, "Follow Me"? (See Matthew 4:18-22.)
Choose a town nearby; it is especially interesting if you choose a town that is a local rival to yours.	• if you had a dream about the kids in the next town crying out to you, "Come on over to _____ and help us"? (See Acts 16:7-10.) • if someone told you, "If you go to the next state, God has told me that you will be persecuted"? (See Acts 21:10-14.) • if God appeared to you in a dream and told you to go talk with the meanest, toughest, roughest kid in town because he had just become a Christian? (See Acts 9:10-19.)

SESSION OUTLINE | TIPS FOR LEADERS

Missions Roulette (10-15 minutes)

Say to students: **Today we are going to imagine that we are God's missions strategists, working to send people out all over the world. After you get into groups of three, I am going to come around with a world globe. I will spin the globe and ask one of you to pinpoint a spot on it. If you land in the water, we'll pick the nearest country or island. If you land on the United States, we'll spin again. After you get your "place," then your group must write a job description for missionaries needed for that part of the world. Remember factors like language, culture, climate, etc.**

It might be good to have a book like *The World Christian Encyclopedia* (Oxford Press) handy to help get some information on countries that you know nothing about.

WORKOUT

20th-Century Update (20 minutes)

Say: **We may not get called by God to go into another culture or around the world, but we must be willing to go if He does direct us. One example of someone whom God called is Jonah. He was reluctant at first, but ultimately he became a very successful missionary.**

Instruct small groups that they will be responsible for an activity that brings Jonah into the 20th century.

Group 1: Read Jonah 1:1-17. This group should make several entries in the journal of Jonah as they might appear if all of this was happening in our time.

Group 2: Read Jonah 1:1-17. This group is to act out these verses with an updated twist to the story.

Group 3: Read Jonah 3:1-10. Do a "man-on-the-street" interview with local Ninevites in which they describe what has been happening in their town.

Group 4: Read Jonah 3:1-10. Assume that the revival in Nineveh has already taken place. This group should feature Jonah on a talk show in which he is describing the events of his life (you should refer to Jonah 1 and 2 as well).

Group 5: Read Jonah 1:1-17 and 3:1-10. Write an article for a contemporary Christian magazine written by Jonah on the subject of "Why you should follow God's call to missions."
  (Tips for the 20th-century update based on the facts of the book:
  1. Jonah is a normal person; he is not a famous person.
  2. Nineveh is a city that Jonah's people would have hated.
  3. Traveling by ship was the most common form of long-distance travel.
  4. Nineveh was a pagan city.)

Make sure leaders read the "Tips" (below) to help make the contemporization effective.

WRAP-UP

The C-A-L-L (10 minutes)

In summary, say: **Many of us are like Jonah; we would rather run from God than go to some difficult place that we would not like. Others, however, say, "I'm willing to go, but I have no idea where, when, or how." The**

A personal testimony from a missionary may be helpful at this point.

| TIPS FOR LEADERS | SESSION OUTLINE |

answer to our fears and our questions lies in a sense of "call" from God. If we understand what He wants us to do, we are most able to follow Him. As you think about God's call on your life, remember these four things:

Prepare a handout beforehand with the letters C-A-L-L down the left side so that your students can complete the acrostic as you speak.

COMMAND: Following Christ is not an optional thing. We must consider our role in His worldwide mission because we are commanded to do so. We should be aware that the greatest needs and opportunities are worldwide. It is far better for us to assume that He wants us to go to "the uttermost parts of the earth" (Acts 1:8) and let Him direct us to stay home.

ABILITY: Many of us are willing to go, but we are afraid that we will fail. Whenever God calls us to serve, He gives the ability. He will give you the ability to leave your loved ones or to learn a new language if He directs you into missions work. Someone has said, "Where God guides, He provides."

LOVE: This is our ultimate motivation to serve others. Jesus loves us, and we love others on His behalf. We start obeying His call by loving the people that He has put in our lives right now. As He directs our steps in the future, He will show us new people whom we should love for His sake.

LORDSHIP: It took Jonah awhile to remember who was really in charge. When we understand that Jesus, not ourselves, controls our lives, we are more willing to submit to Him and say, "Lord, where would you have me go?" If He is our Lord, then we must obey His commands.

When we come down to it, it is that last issue that troubles us most. Jesus is the Lord, but making Him *my* Lord is a difficult decision that I must make every day. And as I do, and as you do, we can see His direction and call on our lives—whether here at home or around the world.

Make sure to make yourself available for students who want to talk about their own personal sense of call to missions.

Close your meeting with prayer (perhaps leaving time for silent prayers of recommitment).

Options for Further Study

Option 1—Have a panel discussion of pastors and missionaries on the subject of "How did God call you into your work?"

Option 2—Start a discussion on a group missions project, or you may (if there is already interest) want to use this session as recruitment.

Additional Resources

Inter-Cristo (P.O. Box 33487, Seattle, WA 98133)
A Christian placement service that does a personal study called "Futures" for high schoolers regarding missions and Christian service.

Stop the World, I Want to Get On (C. Peter Wagner, Regal)
A helpful tool for understanding where an individual can fit in God's plan.

Teen Missions International (P.O. Box 1056, Merritt Island, FL)
Offers summer mission teams for junior highers and high schoolers.

You Can Make a Difference! (Tony Campolo, Word)
A motivational film series (and book).

How to Plan, Develop, and Lead a Youth Mission Team (Paul Borthwick, Grace Chapel, Lexington, MA)
A booklet for leaders on the details of sending a group out on a service project.